Hullo!
Good day.

Where are you going?

Are you growing?

Where are you now?

Where were you five years ago?

Where were you ten years ago?

Your Dream
is Calling You

Veli Ndaba

Copyright ©Veli Ndaba 2016

All rights reserved. No part of this publication may be reproduced, stored in a retrieval system or transmitted in any form or by any means without the prior permission of the publishers.

veli@velindaba.co.za

ISBN 978-0-620-72804-1

Cover design by Angry Monkey Design & Print (Pty) Ltd, www.angrymonkey.co.za Editing & proofreading by Eulália Snyman (Alberton)

Graphics & page layout by Angry Monkey Design & Print (Pty) Ltd (Springs) Printed by Business Print, www.businessprint.co.za (Pretoria)

Photograph by Photo Maria Studio A South African publication

Endorsement

"I first met Veli when he was a member of a mastermind group with Les Brown. During the year that we worked together I was impressed by his spirit, drive, determination and inquisitive mind. In this book, he shares his insights about how to achieve your dreams. You matter. Your dreams matter. Answer the call on your life. We are all waiting for you to shine. This book will show you the way forward."

Vincent Toran, international speaker and trainer, president of Toran Enterprises, LLC. Former corporate executive with years of experience in human resources, marketing, and leadership development.

....

"This is a pragmatic, well written and user friendly book that can be read by anyone including those with a limited attention span like me! The book radiates Veli's passion to continuous development, challenging the status quo and aiming higher to reach one's full potential.

Congratulations Veli, I am confident that this book is going to change lives by unleashing potential in each one of them!"

Julia Modise, seasoned HR professional with 17 years experience, gained locally and internationally in various industries including retail, manufacturing, distribution & properties.

....

"Veli Ndaba has done it again! And he pulls no punches, getting very personal in the process. If you want to be the best you, dig deep and attack those demons. You are the only one holding yourself back from achieving whatever it is that keeps you impassioned.

Your Dream is Calling You is a logical follow-on to Ndaba's first book, *You Are Born to Win*. This time, Ndaba helps us understand all those nuances that hold us back from achieving the greatness in each of us, and offers practical, achievable, realistic and inspiring anecdotes and activities to not only identify your dreams and aspirations, but also to achieve them.

A great read, and certainly beneficial. This will become my new daily go- to book for when I need guidance and inspiration."

Phillip Kassel, CFP® executive financial advisor - Bruma Agency

About Veli

Veli Ndaba was born and bred in Soweto, South Africa. He studied at the University of South Africa [Bachelor of Science in Management Science] and at the University of Johannesburg [National Diploma in Mechanical Engineering] and embarked on a career in the corporate world.

Through hard work and dedication, he soon reached managerial level. However, he felt something was amiss. "I did not feel alive. It was as if something was suffocating me, and I knew I had to make a change. After all, if we do not move forward, life will just move on without us," he says. In 2011 he started his own business, specialising in corporate training, life and business coaching. He joined communication and leadership organisation Toastmasters, eventually became president of his local club and now gives motivational talks around the country. 'Your dream is calling' is Veli's second book.

Veli Ndaba lives in Alberton, a town situated about 20 kms from Johannesburg. He is a family man; he is married to Mpumi and has two sons, Ntokozo and Sanele.

Contact Veli via email veli@velindaba.com or via LinkedIn, Facebook and Twitter.

Disturb us Lord

By Sir Francis Drake [1540 – 1596]

Disturb us, Lord, when
We are too pleased with ourselves, When our dreams have come true Because we dreamed too little,
When we arrived safely
Because we sailed too close to the shore.

Disturb us, Lord, when
With the abundance of things we possess
We have lost our thirst
For the waters of life;
Having fallen in love with life,
We have ceased to dream of eternity
And in our efforts to build a new earth,
We have allowed our vision of the new Heaven to dim.

Disturb us, Lord, to dare more boldly,
To venture on wilder seas
Where storms will show
Your mastery;
Where losing sight of land,
We shall find the stars.

We ask you to push back
The horizons of our hopes;
And to push back the future
In strength, courage, hope, and love.

This we ask in the name of our Captain,
Who is Jesus Christ.

Contents

INTRODUCTION	9
DARE TO DREAM	12
DEVELOPING MASTERY	19
UNDERSTANDING HUMAN NEEDS	30
THE THREE ZONES	44
YOU NEED TO KNOW	44
BUILDING SELF-ETEEM	50
LEARNING A NEW SKILL	59
THE 'WORRY' FACTOR	69
PERSISTENCE MEANS KEEP GOING	77
BE CAREFUL WHAT YOU WISH FOR	83
DEALING WITH FEAR AND RISK	89
CHEERS TO YOUR SUCCESS	101
HOW TO FIND YOUR LIFE'S PURPOSE	106
SOME WHO'VE ANSWERED THE CALL	118
A NOTE ON DREAMING	131
ACKNOWLEDGEMENTS	132
REFERENCES AND SUGGESTED READING	134

Introduction

A higher level of living and being

"The opposite of courage in our society today is not cowardice, it's conformity, wanting to fit in."
– Rollo May (1909 – 1994), an American existential psychologist and author of the influential book 'Love and Will'

Many of us are not happy with our lives, not because of what we don't have but simply because of what we think we need to have. We are unhappy with ourselves, not because of who we are, but because of who we think we should rather be.

We are made to believe that we should be like everyone else. The truth is that we are all pretty different. Like fruit, we humans come in different colours, flavours and packaging. Like fruit, we fulfill different purposes – there's nothing like an orange to quench thirst; nothing like a banana to give a boost of energy. How can we ever believe that sameness is key to having a good life?

We find life dreary, not because we don't have dreams, but because we are chasing other people's dreams. What makes you feel fulfilled, makes you feel that life is worth every breath you take, is probably very different to what floats my boat.
I am here to remind you that your dream is calling you.
I am here to remind you that to really live and feel truly alive you need to answer that call. You need to follow your dream.

Know this: what often holds us back is other people's opinions and expectations of us. Today's society puts much pressure on who we should be, should do and should have. These expectations and opinions are mostly incongruent with who we are and what we are passionate about. The voice of society often deafens our inner voice, making us feel frustrated and as though we are not good enough.

To me, your dream is about what you have to become in order to serve your purpose here on earth. Your dream is associated with becoming the best you, not just having things. What would you do if the highest shelf in a bookcase held the book that has step-by-step instructions of how to be the best? I am sure you would do whatever it took to climb up to get the book.

So for me, becoming 'taller' or reaching higher is key. The book won't drop down onto your lap. Becoming is an intentional act, it's deliberate. It's extremely important to know that success is not something you pursue, but something you attract by becoming attractive, said Jim Rohn. The point I am making here, is that you have to know the truth about what you want in life because without this truth, whatever you want will forever elude you. That's why most people end up blaming their circumstances and other people when they don't get what they want.

We hold ourselves back when we are not true to ourselves and by this I mean we are driven by external factors and the expectations of others. There's friction between what we want and what society expects of us. Knowing what you want is the first step towards the best you. And when you become the best you, you can influence others to be their best.

When you reach your dreams, you inspire others to reach theirs. And this in turn serves to change humanity; it elevates us all to a newer, better, higher level of living and being.

Easier said than done? It may be easier said than done, I agree. But we have to start somewhere. In the pages that follow, I have put together information, inspiration, success stories and practical tools and tips that should help you move towards your dreams and your life purpose.

Make no mistake, I don't have all the answers to the big questions in life. I don't have a magic wand to make your dreams come true. But I have learnt a couple of things that I'd like to share with you in this book. Sometimes I repeat them, sometimes I tackle them from a slightly different angle, gently guiding you towards your dreams.

Dare to dream

"If a 100 foot oak tree had a mind of a human, it would only grow to be 10 feet tall."

Siberian huskies are dogs that Eskimos use for transportation. Because these dogs are so strong, hardy and intelligent, they are trained to follow instructions with precision. When their handlers give them instructions (go forward, turn left and turn right), they follow them with perfect precision.

The challenge with these Siberian huskies comes when they are not given instructions. They simply sit, get bored and cannot do anything by themselves. They are only useful when given instructions to carry out.

Human beings - you and I - use our intelligence; we don't just follow instructions. We're totally different from dogs and all other species on the planet, thank you Lord Creator. We have dreams. We have an inner voice that guides us to be the best we can be. Some people, however, ignore that voice and carry out instructions from others for the rest of their lives. You hear people saying, "I am bored, I don't know what to do, people don't like me, when the time is right I will do such and such." How can you be bored when there's so much to do? When you have not even taken the time to listen to your heart, to find your purpose

in life! The two main things you need to have in order to be happy in life are:
1. Goal (where you are going) and 2. The will to pursue it. Where there is a will there is a way, you have heard of that, and let me tell you it is 100% true.

If you don't know where you are going, someone else will take you wherever he/she wants. So, make time to listen to the voice within, the only guiding light you have. Then you will wave goodbye to your handlers, to boredom, and to the bothersome CBC brothers, namely Complaining, Blaming and Criticising.

Believe in your own dreams and in the fact that you were born to make them come true, no matter what. Your dreams will give your life meaning and confidence. Ignore naysayers. Ignore noise - people telling you that you can't do it, it's hard, you are too short, too tall, you are not clever, you don't have the right colour, and so on. Your dream will help you stay focused against these baseless opinions.

We all have 24 hours in a day, 365 days a year (366 - in a leap year) and how you structure your time is up to you. Be honest with yourself and do simple calculations on how many hours every day you spend investing in yourself. I mean reading books (especially autobiographies and self-help books), attending classes, attending coaching and mentorship programs, listening to audio CDs and networking sessions. Your success in life is mainly a reflection of how many of the 24 hours (subtract the nine hours you spend at work) you spend investing in yourself. Try to account for every hour of your time; try to make every moment count.

If you surround yourself with people who are negative, toxic and energy draining, you will end up exactly like them. The negative talk and complaining you keep on hearing over and over again becomes your reality and subconsciously you will end up just like them. You will exist just to organise pity parties.

To develop a winning mentality, you must always stand guard at the door of your mind! Don't let anyone poison your mind with their negative stuff. No one has a right to feed you negative stuff without your consent.

It is time for you to ask yourself the important question about your relationships. Ask: "What is this relationship doing for me?" Be very clear in your mind what you want to achieve and work hard towards achieving it and you will attract it. That's why it is said that whenever the student is ready to learn, the teacher will appear.

When I made a decision to change my life, I started reading motivational books, listened to positive messages (audio CDs in my car while driving), and attended workshops, conferences, seminars and networking sessions. I eventually got to believe that I could achieve what other successful people have achieved.

Every man is free to rise as far as he is able or willing, but the degree to which he thinks determines the degree to which he will rise. The degree to which someone will rise is fully dependent on the level of self-awareness. You see, you will never out-think your level of awareness. If you lack self- awareness of who you really are and what you are really capable of, you will never think higher and greater of yourself and your possibilities.

Raise your level of self-awareness to see who you really are in your heart and soul. See your true gifts, talents, value, and capabilities. As you do so, your thinking will expand and you will find yourself rising above all limits, be they imposed by yourself or by other people or by circumstances.

It seems that every life form on this planet strives towards its maximum potential - except human beings. A tree does not grow to half its potential size and then say, 'I guess that will do.' A tree will drive its roots as deep as possible. It will soak up as much nourishment as it can, stretch as high and as wide as nature will allow, and then look down as if to remind us of how much each of us could become if we would only do all that we can.

Remember, nothing happens until you decide to take action. Anytime is a good time to dream. Don't just sit there like a Siberian husky – dream your heart out and take steps to make the dream come true.

As a people development catalyst - life coach, author, motivational speaker - I get to speak to people from different walks of life and at different levels of life. Many people I speak to claim to be doing allright. I often wonder what this means. Are they really okay? Or are they saying they're okay because society looks down on those who admit weakness? To dream big and to move towards your dreams you need to look after yourself. There are four areas of wellbeing that you should focus on, namely mental, physical, emotional and spiritual.

Focusing on these areas leads to balanced success:
- Mental - feed your mind with good philosophies everyday (read autobiographies, listen to positive messages and good music)
- Physical - take good care of your body (exercise, eat well, rest)

- Emotional - take note of what upsets you and deal with it in a mature way, be aware of what and who lifts your spirits
- Spiritual – stay in touch with the source of your being

These are simple basic steps that lead to healthy and happy living. Get comfortable with these basics so you can take good care of yourself. Thereafter you will be comfortable with generating money, taking good care of your family and making social contributions to make the world better.

When we are kids we hear advice like, "Be careful, you are gonna get hurt!" or "Watch out, you will be embarrassed, you will fail!"
In our families we are told to be like our brothers and sisters, or other family members. At school we are told to be like other kids. At work we are told to be like other employees.

I really have a problem with this because we are all born to be unique and different, we have different talents and gifts to make this world a better place. Yet, the way we are raised seems to indicate that we must be the same.

We are born to succeed, but unfortunately we are tamed (domesticated) not to reach the pinnacle of our potential by being told that we have to be like others and that failure is the most embarrassing and horrible thing ever. So, I am saying to you, it's time to free yourself by following your heart (if you will fail along the way, it's fine) and listen to that voice of reason deep down in your soul and know from now on that it is acceptable to be yourself, to unleash the power that God has given to you and make this world a much better place. You are unique and special, so be yourself and not somebody else's copy.

Tools & inspiration
Three steps to claim your greatness

"The greatness of a man is not in how much wealth he acquires, but in his integrity and his ability to affect those around him positively." Bob Marley (1945 – 1981), Jamaican musician

Step1
As a human-being, you are born with dignity, you are worthy, your life counts and your life has ultimate significance - meaning you were born for a particular reason. God created you the way you are for a particular reason and purpose. Never be made to feel less than anyone else because of your looks, family background, education, skin colour, nationality, and whatever else makes you unique. That's how God wanted you to be, just be at peace with it and the day you understand this, will be the day you appreciate your
specialness and uniqueness. This should be the basis for living a fulfilling life.

Step 2
Reach for excellence. Make it your way of life to do what you do like nobody else does it. Be the one who turns everything you touch, into gold, as the proverb says. If you look at your job for instance, stop looking at it as just a job, start looking at it as your craft. It's not a secret that the vast majority of people love Fridays and hate Mondays; they hate mornings and love afternoons, the knock-off time. This is simply because they see their jobs as punishment, not as a craft and a gift. People who are experts in what they do, see their jobs as a craft, not something to run away from. The job you are in, is a transition for you to the next big

thing and you will be measured on how well you did or performed in it, so do it well.

Step 3

Look at people who have done wonderful things with their lives and those who are still doing great things. Don't look at these wonderful men and women of substance as exceptions because this will automatically put you at a disadvantage or place of powerlessness. See them as examples of what is possible for you to achieve. Study and copy their daily habits and, trust me on this, your life will never ever be the same again because success and greatness follow a proven pattern.

You are God's special assignment and I truly believe in your greatness, let's do this!

Developing mastery

"Only one who devotes himself to a cause with his whole strength and soul can be a true master. For this reason mastery demands all of a person."
Albert Einstein (1879 – 1955), theoretical physicist who published the special and general theories of relativity

In today's world of hacks, shortcuts and instant money-making blueprints, I think we have lost appreciation for slow-brewing mastery in our work.

We want to become masters overnight, easily earn a title like master chef or braai master like on TV. In real life things work a little differently.

Through the years, I have worked with many great people, leaders and business mentors who have taught me that trying to finish first in a short race is not only stressful, but it also prevents your developing deep expertise and fulfilling purpose.

Purpose is the answer to why we do anything; the reason why you wake up in the morning and do what you do. To live a meaningful and rewarding life, your purpose must be something much bigger than yourself and lead you to deeper joy and resilience. The hallmark of being purposeful is sustaining commitment. Purpose is like a compass, a guiding light and sustained passion in a focused direction.

Watching athletics on TV the other day, I was reminded of what happens when we don't focus or pay attention: an athlete ran fabulously fast and came first – but the judges disqualified him for running in the wrong lane! His speed and efforts didn't count for anything. It was heartbreaking.

So many people are like this athlete, they keep running at the speed of lightning, but because they are all over the show, they don't get anywhere. They may have entertainment value to the watching audience, but they don't achieve their dreams or fulfill their purpose.

If the race represents life and the lane represents your purpose, please focus on choosing your race and running in the correct lane. Don't try to please the spectators in the race of life and don't worry about what the other runners are doing. Be yourself. Run your own race. Chase your own dream. Fulfill your own purpose. You attract what you are, not what you want. And what you are is determined by your beliefs, not your physical body. You can instantly decide to reprogram and redirect your life toward the level of happiness, success and health that you prefer.

So, move away from the place of powerlessness and take your rightful position. Complaining, blaming and criticising are time wasters and dream killers.

My friend, the time to give that dying dream of yours a mouth-to-mouth resuscitation is now. There may be blood, sweat and tears on the way to achieve your dream. I must admit I am full of scars myself. But it's worth it and I keep going. Most of us have heard of the phrase, "You can run, but you cannot hide." That's so true. When you run away from your challenges and let it become a habit to do so, one day your challenges will catch up and have their way with you.

One afternoon I asked my two boys (Ntokozo and Sanele) how their day was, as we always do when we reconnect after work and school. The older one, Ntokozo who is in grade 10, said, "Daddy, you won't believe how many kids have left our accounting and pure mathematics class! They have all taken other subjects that are much easier even though they know this means they won't be able to get into university when they finish school."

This was the first week of the third quarter, they had just returned from (June) winter holidays. Notice how kids that are capable of great things, still choose the easy route and not necessarily the best route.

I said to them, "Boys, once you get used to running away from things and situations in life, it becomes a habit. You may try to run away from difficulties but one day you will run against the wall signaling the end of the road.

Whatever you run away from, will slowly get closer to you and eventually it will catch up with you." I further said to them that we, Ndabas, don't run away from our fears, we confront them head on.

My boys and I (and my wife too) then adopted the mantra, "If you do what is easy, life will be hard for you later; but if you do what is hard, life will be much better for you later." We remind one another of this truth and we encourage each other when we see that the going is tough. We support one another in hitting what we call our personal bull's-eye.

Let me tell you about bull's-eye and the game of darts...

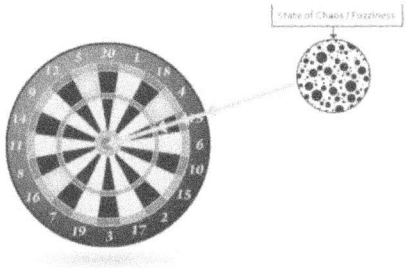

There are many games that can be played on a dartboard, but darts generally refers to a game whereby the player throws three darts per visit to the board with the goal of reducing a fixed score, commonly 501 or 301, to zero ("checking out"), with the final dart landing in either the bull's-eye or a double segment.

To me the dartboard is a representation of how we should live our lives. We need to aim for the bull's-eye. This bull's-eye for me represents living our purpose. When you dream of becoming the best that you can be, there is no reason you cannot become the best.

I am certain you have heard of the saying, 'To be a jack of all trades and a master of none.' This is someone who tries to do everything equally well and ends up mastering none. Mastery is about focus and giving something your full attention; it is about channeling your effort and energy to a particular desired end. It is about picking one thing or area from the state of fuzziness which in this instance is the outside of the dartboard. When you hit the outside of the dartboard, you do not get any points whatsoever, meaning the fixed score of 501 or 301 does not reduce. I am sure you can agree with me in that landing your dart outside the dartboard leads to frustration and despair; it is a waste of time, energy and effort.

To improve your life, pick one thing that your heart desires, work on that tirelessly and ignore what other people say. One of the tools I used in changing my life was to read the following words by Napoleon Hill; I read them with power and conviction and I still read them to this day, to maintain my focus.

They are as follows:

"I ask not, oh divine providence, for more riches, but for more wisdom with which to accept and use wisely the riches given to me at birth; in the form of the power to control and direct my mind to whatever ends I may desire."

Napoleon Hill (October 26, 1883 – November 8, 1970) was an American author best-known for his book Think and Grow Rich (1937). Hill was an advisor to two presidents of the United States of America, Woodrow Wilson and Franklin Roosevelt. His words are profound and remind me that all of us are born rich - not with money, but with the power to focus on our gifts and be so good at them that the money comes flowing our way. All of us have the ability and power to choose one thing and give it everything. To me this is hitting the bull's- eye; where peace of mind, tranquility, fulfillment and higher-self are found.

You have to understand and have patience in your approach, understand that you don't just hit the bull's-eye. The journey starts from outside the dartboard. You start focusing and practising your throws until you can get your darts to hit the target. I am aware that you can hit the bull's-eye right away (beginner's luck, we call it), but to be sustainable, to hit it time and time again, you need to practise.

When you can control your movements and be deliberate about them, it means you can hit wherever you want whenever you want. You don't just throw the dart and hope it hits the bull's-eye, you control your throws and hit the mark as per your aim.

I cannot emphasise enough how important it is to continue practising and improving – whether it's a game of darts, mastering mathematics, controlling your temper, climbing the corporate ladder at work, becoming a kinder person, the list goes on.

When you don't like or are not good at something, use the word yet. "I don't like this yet," leaves room for change. "I am not good at this yet," gives space for

improvement. It's a good trick. It works because it tells your mind to believe that you're almost there.

What distinguishes a hero or a heroine from others is that they face huge challenges that most people are not willing to face. By the time a movie - or real life story - comes to an end, heroes are full of blood, bruises, sweat, tears, torn clothes, exhausted and more often than not, alone. A story only qualifies as

Big, Classic or Powerful when the protagonist triumphs over a huge challenge. This is true with our lives; your dreams will never come to pass without you making serious sacrifices. Ralph Waldo Emerson said, "God will never allow his work to be made manifest by cowards." Dr Martin Luther King Jnr said, "The ultimate measure of a man is not where he stands in moments of comfort and convenience, but where he stands at times of challenge and controversy."

Whether you like it or not, you are creating a story with how you live your life every day and that story will be told to coming generations when you are gone. The story you are busy creating right now is either a comedy, fiction, horror, tragedy or a classic.

If you always want convenience and comfort and are busy complaining about how unfair life is towards you, you are definitely not creating a classic or powerful story. Why not just choose to create a powerful story?

You are not a mistake or born to play small. God said 'Yes' to your life long before you were conceived. You were born to make your life count and something as powerful as you cannot be contained or stopped. You may be delayed along the way, but not stopped. You are meant to fulfill your purpose on earth. You are meant to achieve your dreams (if these are for your good and the good of others, of course). God has made you the master of your life.

Tools & inspiration
Developing mastery

"I never learned a thing from a tournament I won."
Bobby Jones (1902 – 1971), American amateur golfer, and a lawyer by profession

1. Learn patience

My late aunt used to say we shouldn't rush to finish something, because if you rush you don't get to enjoy it. Even when we were cooking and eating food she wouldn't allow us to rush it, she would tell us to slow down and enjoy the food. For her, eating was not merely about filling your tummy. In essence, she meant the journey was much more important than just rushing to reach the destination. She used to say that patience leads to happiness and satisfaction in knowing you took the time to do something well – even if it's just eating. I learned a lot from this lesson and am applying it in my life as a professional speaker, author, life-coach and other areas of my life as I understand that good things do not happen overnight. Every new skill you learn can lead to frustration without this element of patience. When you apply this technique in your life you will appreciate how you engage with your task at hand while learning the insights of your craft.

2. Practise the basics

When we first learn a new skill, we dive into it with everything we have, taking classes, learning from mentors and practising like crazy. When we reach a certain level of success, we often get lazy. True masters never stop practising the basics. Martial artists do push ups and sit ups every day of their lives. Artists practise brush strokes. Writers write daily. Entrepreneurs create, market and sell. When you don't practise the basics, they go away.

3. Appreciate the source of your materials

I once watched a documentary called Jiro Dreams of Sushi. Jiro Dreams of Sushi, is the story of 85-year-old Jiro Ono, considered by many to be the world's greatest sushi chef. He is the proprietor of Sukiyabashi Jiro, a 10-seat, sushi-only restaurant inauspiciously located in a Tokyo subway station. Despite its humble appearances, it is the first restaurant of its kind to be awarded a prestigious three-star Michelin Guide rating, and sushi lovers from around the globe make repeated pilgrimages, calling months in advance and shelling out top dollar for a coveted seat at Jiro's sushi bar. In Jiro Dreams of Sushi, Jiro's son walks slowly around the fish market, looking for the perfect fish for the evening meals. He has relationships with fishermen who will not sell their product to anyone but him. Great work is built with great materials, by people and partners who care as much about what they do as you care about what you do. Avoid cheap, sloppy and poorly constructed source materials. I am also referring to relationships you have as they form part of your sources, so always choose well.

4. Deconstruct everything

Often, success is random. If you started a business some years ago, you might have thought you were naturally talented. The market was flourishing. Companies were throwing huge sums of money around for training, employee perks and expensive toys. If you do well, take the time to figure out exactly what were the conditions that led to your success.

If you have a raging failure, figure out exactly which conditions, personal and environmental, led to your failure. As Don Miguel Ruiz says in The Four Agreements, "Don't take things personally. Nothing others do is because of you. What others say and do is a projection of their own reality, their own dreams."

5. Set boundaries

You cannot create great work if you are in a constant state of reaction. You must protect your creative work time by blocking out your schedule, turning off your phone and closing down your email. You must protect your creative energy by avoiding "life sucking squids," as Martha Beck calls people who only care about their own edification and not about your needs or soul. As Eleanor Roosevelt said, "No one can take advantage of you without your permission." Create your moment of silence and connect with your deeper soul.

6. Make your space holy

When you respect your work, you want to create a beautiful, clean, sacred container for it. Regardless of the size, cost or fanciness of your physical space, treat it with reverence. Pay attention to what you bring into it. Take time to clean the floor and wash the windows. Surround yourself with images of beauty and inspiration. Give gratitude to the tools that you use to do your work, and to all the masters who have come before you.

7. Cultivate your voice

While you can become fluent in another language, you will never feel more anchored and at home than when you are speaking your native tongue.

Explore your voice. Listen to your intuition. Write down your thoughts. Develop your ideas. Don't get distracted by your love for someone else's voice.

8. Swallow your pride

True mastery is based on a love affair with your work. You want to take a great photograph, or write a great paragraph, or lead a transformational coaching event because you want to make the profession proud. You want to please the past masters and the art itself. If your work is criticised, or isn't up to your own standards, don't take it personally. If you receive lots of accolades and exposure, don't let it get to your head. Keep your focus on honouring your profession.

9. Punch through the bag

If you just focus on hitting the target itself, your punch will be weak. Set your target a few millimeters behind the punching bag, and aim to hit that. The same applies to your work. How does today's goal relate to tomorrow's goal, and next year's goal? How will your choices today affect your relatives in seven generations? Always think ahead.

10. When imitated, innovate

When you are great at what you do, people are bound to imitate you. Sometimes they will try to steal your intellectual property, or students, or employees or business model, or artistic genre. It is natural to get upset when this happens. But instead of fighting with the imitator, move on to innovate the next stage of your work. If you are doing your job well, your work is constantly improving and growing. Imitate that.

Once you begin to cultivate a mastery mind-set, life slows down and you appreciate the delicious nuances in every moment.

11. Remember: Your purpose should be bigger than yourself.

To be yourself in a world that is constantly seeking to make you something else is the greatest achievement.

Understanding human needs

"Wherever your treasure is, there the desires of your heart will also be"
Bobby Jones (1902 – 1971), American amateur golfer, and a lawyer by profession

An old lady stood in her night gown on the pavement at 2 am one morning, staring in stunned disbelief as mighty flames turned her house into a little heap of ashes and smoke. She began to shiver as she thought of her warm bed, tea, slippers and heater. She shivered worse when she thought of all the expensive and priceless belongings that she had devoted her entire life to collecting. What else had she done with her life? Nothing! She had spent it collecting all the things that were now burning to cinders.

Next morning in hospital, all her friends and family came to her bedside to comfort her. Expecting to find her in a terrible state of tears, shock and fear over her loss, they were surprised to find her in the best of spirits, laughing and talking loudly with great excitement - something she had never done as long as they had known her. "She has lost her mind," someone whispered.

But she had not lost her mind. On the contrary she had found it. "I am free!" she exclaimed. "I was trapped in my own prison of precious, priceless belongings. I was afraid to leave the house in case someone broke in. I was afraid to have people over in case they stole, spoiled or broke something. I was suspicious of my children, and afraid they were waiting for me to die so they could inherit my things. I see it all now. I was wasting my life! My belongings made me bitter from getting close to my loved ones. Now I feel so wonderful; I feel so free."

Are you living life the same way as this woman lived hers? Do all your dreams revolve around possessions and positions? Don't feel bad – most of us make the same mistake.

To change our way of thinking, we need to understand human needs and how our human mind works.

Abraham Maslow (April 1, 1908 – June 8, 1970) was an American psychologist known for creating a hierarchy of needs, a theory of psychological health predicated on fulfilling innate human needs in priority, culminating in self-actualisation. Maslow wanted to understand what motivates people. He believed that people possess a set of motivation systems unrelated to rewards or unconscious desires. He stressed the importance of focusing on the positive qualities in people, as opposed to treating them as a "bag of symptoms." Maslow stated that people are motivated to achieve certain needs. When one need is fulfilled, a person seeks to fulfill the next one, and so on.

The earliest and most widespread version of Maslow's (1943, 1954) hierarchy of needs includes five motivational needs, often depicted as hierarchical levels within a pyramid. I believe that kids at primary school nowadays study this pyramid, and I am very glad about that – it's a real eye-opener.

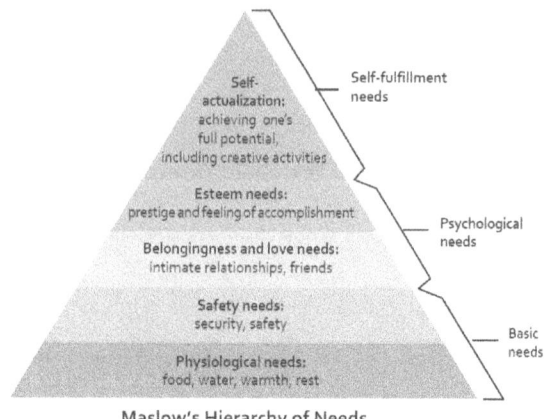

Maslow's Hierarchy of Needs

The five-stage model can be divided into basic and psychological needs which ensure survival and growth needs.

Human needs as identified and arranged by Maslow:

At the bottom of the hierarchy are the "basic needs or physiological needs" of a human being: food, water, sleep and sex.

The next level is "safety needs: security, order, and stability". These are important to the physical survival of the person. Once individuals have basic nutrition, shelter and safety, they attempt to accomplish more.

The third level of need is "love and belonging", which are psychological needs; when individuals have taken care of themselves physically, they are ready to share themselves with others, such as with family and friends.

The fourth level is achieved when individuals feel comfortable with what they have accomplished. This is the "esteem" level, the need to be competent and recognised, such as through status and level of success. Esteem needs include achievement, mastery, independence, status, dominance, prestige, self-respect, and respect from others. Maslow suggests esteem needs take two forms: (a) a need for strength, achievement, mastery and competence; (b) a need for reputation, status, recognition and appreciation. Fulfilment of these needs leads to a sense of self-confidence, worth, and value to the world.

The fifth level is "self-actualisation needs" - realising personal potential, self-fulfilment, seeking personal growth and peak experiences.

Humans must satisfy lower level basic needs before progressing to meet higher level needs. Once these needs have been reasonably satisfied, humans may be able to reach the highest level called self-actualisation.

Every person is capable and has the desire to move up the hierarchy toward a level of self-actualisation. Unfortunately, progress is often disrupted by failure to meet lower-level needs. Life experiences, including divorce and loss of job may cause an individual to fluctuate between levels of the hierarchy.

Maslow noted only one in a 100 people become fully self-actualised because our society rewards motivation primarily based on esteem, love and other social needs.

He describes the good life as one directed towards self-actualisation, the pinnacle need. Self-actualisation occurs when you maximise your potential, doing the best that you are capable of doing. Maslow studied individuals that he believed to be self-actualised, including Abraham Lincoln, Thomas Jefferson, and Albert Einstein, to derive the common characteristics of the self-actualised person. So, who is a self-actualised person, and what characteristics does s/he have? In his book 'Motivation and Personality', he highlights 12 main characteristics of self-actualised humans:

1. Self-actualised people embrace the unknown and the ambiguous.

They are not threatened or afraid of it; instead, they accept it, are comfortable with it and are often attracted by it. They do not cling to the familiar. Maslow quotes Einstein as saying: "The most beautiful thing we can experience is the mysterious."

2. They accept themselves, flaws and all.
They perceive themselves as they are, and not as they would prefer to be. They can accept their own human nature in the tolerant style, with all its shortcomings, with all its discrepancies from the ideal image without feeling real concern. Nonetheless, while self-actualised people are accepting of shortcomings that are immutable, they do feel ashamed or regretful about changeable deficits and bad habits.

3. They prioritise and enjoy the journey, not just the destination.
They often regard as ends in themselves many experiences and activities that are, for other people, only means. Our subjects are somewhat more likely to appreciate for its own sake, and in an absolute way, the doing itself; they can often enjoy for its own sake the getting to some place as well as arriving. It is occasionally possible for them to make out of the most trivial and routine

activity an intrinsically enjoyable game or dance or play.

4. While they are inherently unconventional, they do not seek to shock or disturb.
Unlike the average rebel, self-actualised persons recognise that people cannot understand or accept their unconventionality, and since they have no wish to hurt or to fight with others over triviality, they will go through the ceremonies and rituals of convention with a good-humoured shrug and with the best possible grace. Self-actualised people would usually behave in a conventional fashion simply because no great issues are involved or because they know people will be hurt or embarrassed by a different kind of behaviour.

5. They are motivated by growth, not by the satisfaction of needs.
While most people are still struggling in the lower rungs of the hierarchy of needs, the self-actualised focus on personal growth. They no longer strive in the ordinary, but rather develop. They attempt to grow to perfection and to develop more and more fully in their own style. The motivation of ordinary people is a striving for the basic need gratification that they lack.

6. Self-actualised people have purpose.
They have some mission in life, some task to fulfil, some problem outside themselves which enlists much of their energies. This is not necessarily a task that they would prefer or choose for themselves; it may be a task that they feel is their responsibility, duty, and obligation. In general, these tasks are non-personal or unselfish, concerned rather with the good of mankind in general.

7. They are not troubled by the small things.
Self-actualised people focus on the bigger picture. They seem never to get so close to the trees that they fail to see the forest. They work within the framework of values that are broad and not

petty, universal and not local, and in terms of a century rather than a moment. This impression of being above small things seems to impart a certain serenity and lack of worry over immediate concerns that make life easier not only for themselves but for all who are associated with them.

8. Self-actualised people are grateful.
They do not take their blessings for granted, and by doing so, maintain a fresh sense of wonder towards the universe. Self-actualising people have a wonderful capacity to appreciate again and again, freshly and naively, the basic goods of life, with awe, pleasure, wonder, and even ecstasy, however stale these experiences may have become to others. Thus for such a person, any sunset may be as beautiful as the first one, any flower may be of breath-taking loveliness, even after he has seen a million flowers. For such people, even the
casual workday, moment-to-moment business of living can be thrilling.

9.They share deep relationships with a few, but also feel identification and affection towards the entire human race.
Self-actualised people have deeper and more profound interpersonal relations than other adults. They are capable of more fusion, greater love, more perfect identification, more obliteration of the ego boundaries than other people would consider possible. The devotion exists side by side with a wide spreading benevolence, affection, and friendliness. These people tend to be kind and friendly to almost everyone of suitable character regardless of class, education, political belief, race, or colour.

10. Self-actualised people are humble.
They are all quite well aware of how little they know in comparison with what could be known and what is known by others. Because of this it is possible for them, without pose, to be honestly respectful and even humble before people who can

teach them something.

11. Self-actualised people resist enculturation.

They do not allow themselves to be passively moulded by culture — they deliberate and make their own decisions, selecting what they see as good, and rejecting what they see as bad. They neither accept all, like a sheep, nor reject all, like the average rebel. Self-actualised people make up their own minds, come to their own decisions, are self-starters, are responsible for themselves and their own destinies. Too many people do not make up their own minds, but have their minds made up for them by salesmen, advertisers, parents, propagandists, TV, newspapers and so on.

12. Despite all this, self-actualised people are not perfect and they know it.

There are no perfect human beings! Persons can be found who are good, very good, in fact, great. And yet these very same people can at times be boring, irritating, petulant, selfish, angry, or depressed. To avoid disillusionment with human nature, we must first give up our illusions about it.

The reason I am sharing Abraham Maslow's hierarchy of needs is to indicate to you how the majority of people are stuck at the bottom of the pyramid. The reason why most people are stuck at the bottom is simply because of the wrong expectations and competition that has been created by society. We have been made to believe that conformity is the way to go, that we have to compete on materialistic things that at the end do not bring out the best in us. This only raises the level of ego.

Ego is an unhealthy belief in one's importance because of what one has. Ego is almost the opposite of confidence. When you are stuck at the bottom level of Maslow's hierarchy of needs, your quality of life is based or measured by what you have materialistically.

At these bottom levels one has to always 'appear' to be the best in terms of what he has - expensive clothing, shoes, cars, TV sets, cell phones, houses, and so on. These things, however, do not help one to develop as a strong person; instead they somehow create a lot of anxiety and fear based on the possibility of losing them. Most people end up being possessed by their possessions instead of them possessing their possessions, this is a vicious circle; you end up chasing things that you cannot even afford. Some people for example, carry cell phones that cost more than their monthly salaries. This is a sad truth, but that's how life is.

If you don't have expensive things, then you are considered not-good-enough and poor. At these bottom levels, poverty is defined as a lack of money or credit to acquire these things - hence people become stretched and stressed out and heavily indebted just to keep up with the neighbours or society. People who thrive on accumulation of materialistic things see others as being poor.

To be yourself in a world that is constantly seeking to make you something else is indeed a great achievement. The good news is that it is possible to move up Maslow's hierarchy of needs. It is also possible to stand your ground and stay true to yourself, your values and your dreams. You needn't give in to society's pressure and you can resist even the most subtle of conditioning ploys.

What is conditioning? In the early twentieth century, Ivan Pavlov (1839 – 1948), Russian physiologist, did Nobel prize-winning work on digestion. While studying the role of saliva in dogs' digestive processes, he stumbled upon a phenomenon he labelled "psychic reflexes."

While this was an accidental discovery, he had the foresight to see the importance of it. Pavlov's dogs, restrained in an experimental room, were presented with meat powder and they had their saliva collected via a surgically implanted tube in their

saliva glands. Over time, he noticed that his dogs began salivating before the meat powder was
even presented, whether it was by the presence of the handler or merely by a clicking noise produced by the device that distributed the meat powder. Fascinated by this finding, Pavlov paired the meat powder with the ringing of a bell.

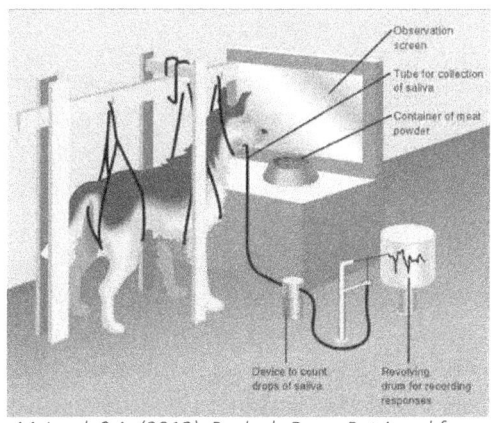

McLeod, S.A. (2013). Pavlov's Dogs. Retrieved from www.simplypsychology.org/pavlov.html.

After the meat powder and bell (auditory stimulus) were resented together several times, the bell was used alone. Pavlov's dogs, as predicted, responded by salivating to the sound of the bell (without the food). The bell began as a neutral stimulus (the bell itself did not produce the dogs' salivation). However, by pairing the bell with the stimulus that did produce the salivation response, the bell was able to acquire the ability to trigger the salivation response. Pavlov therefore demonstrated how stimulus- response bonds (which some consider as the basic building blocks of learning) are formed.

I find it fascinating that the dogs learned to associate the bell with food and started salivating even if the food was not presented or seen by them. The mere ringing of the bell just got them salivating.

This also happens with human beings. We see an advertisement, and, like Pavlov's dogs at the ringing of bells, we start salivating. What you watch on television, hear on radio, see in newspaper adverts, hear people talking about and displaying, are stimuli or unrealistic needs presented to us all the time. If you don't have your own dream, purpose and goals, you will surely behave like Pavlov's dogs and run after every bell you hear ringing - even if there's nothing on the other side.

Having the best TV set, best shoes, best food, best cars, best clothing and so on, promotes ego which is about accumulating and having things at the expense of being the best human being that you can be. Remember that ego is about positions and things that you may lose at any time, whereas confidence is about the person you are, which is the result of a deliberate self-development process. Fortunately human beings are endowed with intelligence to question things, set goals and plan whatever they desire. We are not Pavlov's dogs. We can set goals and plans to achieve such goals. We have faith and imagination to take us where we haven't been before.

Yes, don't ever underestimate the role of faith and imagination when it comes to becoming the best you and achieving dreams. Faith is the act of seeing the finish line in the mental realm before it is manifested in the physical. Faith is believing things that do not yet exist in the physical, will one day exist. Here is that 'yet' word again, see?

Everything starts with creative imagination. You can only achieve in life what you can see in your imagination. If you cannot imagine it, forget it. Albert Einstein said, "Imagination is the preview of what's to come." Imagination connects you to a bigger and better part of you. You need to set meaningful goals in order to achieve what you have imagined; goal-setting becomes key.

Failure to set goals and act on them leads to low self-esteem, unhappiness, self-hate, fear and guilt. Without setting goals you will face your future with apprehension or fingers crossed hoping that things work out well for you, without your control.

Tools & inspiration
Imagine a better life, a better you

"To be yourself in a world that is constantly trying to make you something else is the greatest achievement."
Ralph Waldo Emerson (1803 – 1882), American essayist, lecturer and poet

The following four steps, in the order they are stated, will lead to a meaningful life of substance, pride and joy:

1. Imagine a meaningful life and future
2. Set goals to bring your imagination to reality
3. Take action on your goals
4. Have faith that you will achieve your dreams. Always remember, it's not
5. the size of the dog in the fight, it's the size of the fight in the dog that will determine the results.

The story of Kenneth Behring

Kenneth Eugene Behring (born June 13, 1928) is a famous American real estate tycoon and former owner of the American National Football League's Seattle Seahawks. His life went through four stages:

- **Getting stuff** – acquiring a lot of money, big house, expensive cars, yacht, collection of wines all over the world, and so on, but still was not happy.
- **Getting better stuff** – upgrading to better stuff. He acquired more expensive things, still he wasn't happy.
- **Getting different stuff** – he bought the Seattle SeaHawks team (football team), still he wasn't happy.
- **Finding purpose** – one day he and his friend decided to fly to Bosnia to donate some wheelchairs.

When they got there they started picking up kids and putting them on the wheelchairs. The first kid he picked up was about 11 years old and when he tried to put him in the wheelchair, the kid held on to him and wouldn't let go. Through an interpreter the child said "Please don't go yet, I want to look at your face to memorise it so that when we meet again in heaven I can thank you again." Behring started to cry uncontrollably; for the first time in his life he felt pure joy. After that incident, he started a wheelchair foundation, which has, so far, donated over 400 000 wheelchairs to children all over the world.

He has written a book called 'Life's Purpose' in which he talks about the real joy that comes from giving. He says it's critical to make a lot of money because money is very useful; without money the good you can do is limited to your physical presence.

Remember: Your purpose should be bigger than yourself; going beyond your own concerns, answering a bigger 'why' automatically increases your power, energy and resilience.

The three zones you need to know

"It's not enough to be in the right place at the right time, you have to be the <u>right person</u> in the <u>right place</u> at the <u>right time</u>!"
T. Harv Erker (1954 -), author of the book 'Secrets of the Millionaire Mind'

We've all heard of the comfort zone, but do you know about the two other zones? And do you know in which zone you are at present?
If you get stuck in a zone, you cannot move towards your dream. So it's imperative that you stop every once in a while, smell the roses and ask yourself if you are moving in the right direction. One of the best ways to do that is to look at each of the following three zones and ask yourself which one you're living in:

1. The comfort zone
2. The stretch/learning zone
3. The snap/panic zone

Zone 1: The comfort zone
The comfort zone is where many of us operate. It's the zone where we are safe and secure. This is a zone we think we want to

live in, after all who doesn't want to be safe and secure? But this zone is not in our best interest in the long term.

We can't make progress or build skills in the comfort zone since it consists of the abilities we already have. So, how do you know you are stuck in this zone, you may ask? You know you're in this zone when you're bored, when you are not feeling any challenge. At first you don't realise you're bored, of course. It seeps into your soul unannounced, but it's boredom just the same.

Zone 2: The stretch zone
This zone is found just a step outside your comfort. This zone has nothing to do with maintaining the status quo. The Stretch zone is "walking naked into the land of uncertainty," according to leadership guru Robert Quinn. The skills and abilities that are just out of reach are in the learning zone; they're neither so far away that we panic nor close enough where they're too easy.

You know you're in this zone when you're a little excited and a little scared, at the same time. You're in this zone when you have big dreams for the future. Dreams you can almost taste and touch, but don't know exactly how you'll achieve. And that's okay, you'll figure it out. This is when you have to walk by faith and not by sight. This is when the excitement of winning is your main driver and fear of losing is starving to death.

Zone 3: The snap/panic zone
In this zone, we experience an intense tiredness that doesn't go away. Our sleep isn't restful; and when we awake, we're not refreshed. With this fatigue also comes an emotional weariness, a lingering sadness that has no real loss associated with it. If you've ever become so anxious you can no longer think, you've probably run into the panic zone.

Activities in the panic zone are so tough that we don't even know how to approach them. The overall feeling of the panic zone is that you are uncomfortable and possibly discouraged. Like the comfort zone, we can't make progress in the panic zone. You may be in the panic zone when attempting something dangerous, far beyond your reach or under high stress.

If you're in this zone, the answer isn't giving up on your vision and going back to the days when you were bored and pathetic. It's just backing off a bit, taking a step back and reflecting. Catch your breath and take some time to reconnect with the true, energetic and creative you.

The panic zone can easily be mistaken as the learning zone. People make this mistake since they've heard "no pain, no gain" many times. However, they're not synonymous and if this were true, the happiest and most successful people would be in lots of pain. While the panic zone and learning zone may involve forms of "pain" and challenges, the panic zone is a place where we are lost, while in the learning zone we are focused and open to new ideas.

Life is about growth, you can either go back to your comfort zone where you won't find any growth or you must be willing to go forward and face your fears again and again and again. There truth is that you will never have a fear-free existence, some fear is acceptable and legitimate. So it's okay to have some fear but don't let it immobilise you. There's a difference between having fear and fear having you. Acknowledge and embrace the fear you have. Don't resist it because whatever you resist, tends to persist.

Purposeful living is a marathon and not a sprint. When running a marathon, pacing is all-important so you can finish well. Just pause right now and take stock and establish which one of these zones are you in right now. The Comfort Zone, the Stretch/Learning Zone, or the Snap/Panic Zone? And what do you need to do about it? Do this from time to time and your life will be exciting and rewarding.

So, if we know that boredom is an indication of the comfort zone, and losing focus or being frantic is indicative of the panic zone, the learning zone is easier to spot. The learning zone can also be thought of as the growth, engaged, or enjoyment zone. When we learn, there's usually a level of engagement or enjoyment. We're neither bored nor uneasy.

We're learning. Identifying what zone you are in and making the necessary adjustments to be in the learning zone will mean consistent progress and growth.

Many of us don't go to the next level of our greatness because of self- doubt and we stay stuck. Greatness is a choice we have to make every day.

By continuously challenging and raising the bar on yourself, you discover parts of you that you never knew...Your dream life happens outside the comfort zone.

Tools & inspiration
Drag yourself out of your comfort zone

"A wise person will always find a way."
Tanzanian proverb

We all have potential, but sadly, some people are under the illusion that it's only for the chosen few. Think of muscles, biceps and triceps in particular. We all have them, but what size and shape they take entirely depends on you, they are yours.

Look at the body builders. They have well-toned and big muscles. They were surely not born that way. All body builders will tell you it takes burning desire, a plan, hard work and commitment to build muscle – there are no short cuts!

A muscle in its natural form is a classic example of potential. Until you develop and work it, it will remain small and weak. Remember your brain is a muscle too. We all have talents (potential), but if not developed or polished, these talents won't shine and will remain dull and unnoticed. So stop wasting time envying other people's muscles: you have yours to shape and size the way you want them.

Never settle for mediocrity in life. Always search for higher ground, you have potential in abundance to do so. Invest in yourself - it is the best investment you can make. It's truly not enough to be in the right place at the right time. Until you start investing in yourself you will not be prepared to recognise that you are the *right person* in the *right place* at the *right time*.

Read positive material continuously, attend seminars, workshops and meet new people with new ideas. In this way you will grow. I call this searching for your destiny.

You can't find something of value if you don't search; the findings are for the seekers. Most people complain that they don't know what their talents are. This simply means they haven't searched enough. Keep searching until you find it and when you do, your heart will tell you if you're right.

Building self-Eteem

"I freed a thousand slaves. I could have freed a thousand more if only they knew they were slaves."
Harriet Tubman (1822 – 1913), American humanitarian, who acted as a spy for US Army during the American Civil War

Seeing yourself as a worthy human being before anything else is the first and the key step to building self-esteem and self-confidence. I don't know where I heard the story below, but I really like it:

*One day a man was watching a football game on television. His five-year-
old son kept bothering him. So the man tore a page from the newspaper. It was a full-page airline advertisement that showed a picture of the world, planet earth as seen from space. He tore the page in dozen pieces and gave them to his son.*
He said, "Here, put this picture together with this tape, and show daddy how smart you are."
He then went back to watching his game.
In a surprisingly short time, the youngster had taped the picture back together. It wasn't very neat, but it was a very good job indeed, for one so young.
"Hey, that's amazing," the father said. "How did you put that

world together so quickly?"
The little boy said, "There was a picture of the man on the other side. I just put the man together, and the world was all together." The youngster got a big, warm hug from his father. "That's right, son," the father said. "When a man is all-together, his world is all-together, too."

The lesson I take from the story is that one should not focus on working and expecting the world to come together, but rather to work on oneself first and then the world will follow suit.

Confidence is the disposition to experience oneself as competent to cope with the basic challenges of life and as being worthy of happiness.

Self-confidence comes as a result of self-acceptance. Self-acceptance is about knowing that you were born for a purpose and that you are unique and special and that your life counts. One of the main reasons some of us have low self-esteem or confidence is what we have been told we are or are not, over and over and over again, in comparison to others. Certain people in our society create this 'standard of acceptance', which unfortunately is misaligned with our own purpose. The society 'standard' of conforming is the one that makes you feel inferior to others; this standard is also very elusive, you really can't keep up with it as there will always be someone 'better' than you. This leads to you feeling you are not good enough.

The vast majority of people lose sight of their dreams because of this society 'standard' to conform and to compete for sameness. Everyone you meet in life will paint you with the colour of their choice if you let them. This happens when you are pleasing people for acceptance: you walk in a certain way, wear certain clothes, listen to certain music and live in a particular place so people will accept you.

It's important to know why you are here on planet earth; what is your purpose? The whole thing about existence or life is living your own life according to your purpose - not to follow the masses. The reason you end up feeling lost and despondent is simply because you live your life according to other people's standards. I invite you to re-discover yourself by listening to your heart. The critical question you need ask yourself is, "If I had not been told what I am good or bad at and were to have my 'bills' taken care of, meaning I had no financial obligations, what would I do with my life?"

Most people I have spoken to, have their creativity drowned out by the lingering thought of paying bills and merely exist instead of living and enjoying life.

Self-esteem has two components to it:

1. Self-efficacy: it is your ability to think for yourself and direct your own life. It's about having confidence that you can create your own life and that you can take care of yourself without relying much on others. If you were to create a scale of one to 10, one being the lowest and 10 being the highest, where do you rank yourself on that scale? Ask yourself that question. If you rank yourself on one it means you cannot do anything by yourself, you always see yourself as a victim, always feeling and thinking that the world is out to get you. You feel crippled and paralysed.

The lower levels of self-efficacy can be best depicted by the following triangle of victimhood called Dreaded Drama Triangle™ as described by David Emerald:

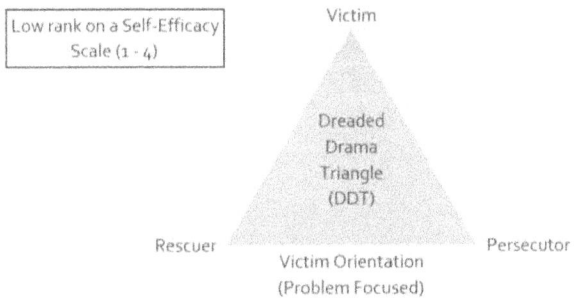

A person with a low level of self-efficacy has a victim orientation and assumes three different roles. These roles are Victim, Persecutor and Rescuer. This position is problem-focused. A person with this victim orientation feels persecuted and attacked by people, things and events in life; he/she takes no responsibility whatsoever.

People with victim mentality feel they have no control over their lives and that the world is out to attack them. From that position they seek for rescue by assuming 'rescuer' persona. They spend time on things that will make them feel better about themselves like Facebook, alcohol, drugs and spend most of their time watching TV, surfing the Internet and many other time wasting non-value adding activities. They get involved in these activities or things just to numb themselves. This victimhood or victim-orientation is not good for you; in it you are a puppet, paralysed and feeling helpless because you see the world as in control, not you. You live life from a place of powerlessness.

If, on the other hand, you rank yourself on the higher levels of the scale (up to 10), it means you feel that you are in full control of your life and you can direct your life where you want without, or with minimal, support from others. When you see yourself on level 10 or close to it, it means you see yourself as a 'creator' and not a victim in life. It means you are able to accept that there will be tough situations in your life in terms of your relationships, career, job, and health, but that you have the capacity to work them out whenever they may arise. This is a positive and healthy approach to life which leads to tranquility and success.

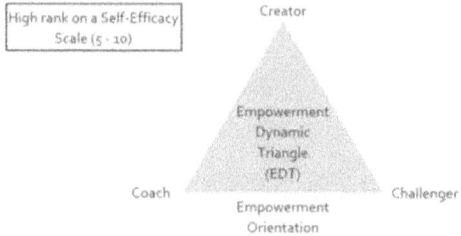

A person represented by this triangle (Empowerment Dynamic Triangle) has the empowerment orientation and feels he is the creator of his future. A creator experiences the same challenges as a victim with a different lens or perspective. Instead of focusing on problems, a creator focuses on the ideal vision, focuses on what s/he wants. If the challenges are beyond him, he ropes in coaches, mentors and people who can help him find answers and get what he wants.

When you are caught in victim mentality, you focus on your problems too much, you really thrive on this. If you are not feeling good about yourself, you are definitely projecting your shadow everywhere you go and this is not good at all.

2. Self-respect: how much do you respect yourself? Do you really believe that you have value as a human being, as you are right now? Do you really believe that you have a right and deserve to be happy? Do you really believe that you deserve to be treated well and with respect? You deserve the best and shouldn't settle for less. These values should be part of your mental blueprint, your philosophy. Rank yourself on a scale of one to 10 in terms of how much you respect yourself, one being the lowest and 10 being the highest. Once again if you rank yourself on one, it means that you have no self-respect. You really don't care about yourself. This means you don't value your happiness and dignity, you consider yourself just as other people's doormat and that people can just do whatever they want with you. People look at you and know how to treat you based on how you treat yourself. On the other hand, if you rank yourself on the highest, it means you see yourself as the most valuable and respectable person on earth. You see yourself as the centre of your life, the most important thing alive. When you respect yourself you don't have to change yourself for people, you accept yourself for who you are and are happy.

So when we talk about self-esteem, it's really about these two important components: self-efficacy and self-respect. It's about how you value yourself. Self-esteem is really believing in who you are. It's not about the world, people and things, but about you. Self-esteem is all about the inner game. It's inside you. If you really believe that you can handle any situation (ranking 10 in self-efficacy) in your life and also respect yourself highly (ranking 10 in self-respect), there's no way you can stay in an abusive relationship or situation that is not aligned to who you see yourself to be.

To see how you are ranked on these two scales, self-efficacy and self- respect, just look at how you handle your personal issues. Once again look at where you are in these scales and it will give you a clear indication in terms of where to start working on building your self-esteem.

Tools & Inspiration
Controlling your self-talk

"When people hurt you over and over, think of them as sandpaper. They scratch you and hurt you, but later, you will be shining and polished, while they end up useless."
Unknown

From the moment you were born, every message you got - everything that you were told, that you heard and that you saw - was saved in your subconscious mind. These things were repeated over and over again until they formed your program. It is this program that drives your beliefs and the way you think which ultimately produce the results you are producing right now.

If you're not happy with your results don't blame other people or circumstances. What you need to do instead is to change your programming. Now, how do you do this? You do this by controlling your self-talk, what you tell yourself on a daily basis. There are five levels of self-talk

Level 1 - The level of negative acceptance
"I can't", "I wish I could, but I can't", "I could never do that", "I can never lose weight." These statements cripple our best intentions and seduce us into becoming satisfied with mediocrity.

Level 2 - The level of recognition and need to change
"I need to," or "I ought to," or "I should," Why does that work

against us? Because it recognises a problem, but creates no solution at all. "I really need to cut down on my smoking", "I've got to do something about that!"

Level 3 - In this level you recognise the need to change, and make the decision to do something about it

You state the decision in the present tense, as though the change has already taken place.

This level is characterised by the words, "I never" or "I no longer." In this level you say, "I never smoke!", "I no longer have a problem dealing with people at work," "I never eat more than I should," "I never get upset in traffic," "I no longer put off doing anything I want to get done." When you move to Level 3, you are automatically beginning to rephrase old negative "cannots," putting them behind you, and stating them in a positive new way that tells your subconscious mind to wake up, get moving, and make the change.

Level 4 - You paint a complete new picture of yourself

This is the kind of self-talk that is used the least and is needed most: "This is the me I want you to create! Forget all that bad programming I gave you in the past. Mind, this is your new program. I am a winner! I am healthy,
energetic, enthusiastic, and I'm going for it! Nothing can stop me now. I like who I am."

Level 5 - You recognise yourself as a worthy human being

"I can do anything, I allow myself choices, I can say no, I am not perfect but I am perfectly me."

Listen to yourself every time you talk to yourself and start upgrading your self-talk level. Positive self-talk is a proven way to re-write your programming and make your dreams come true.

Always remember that our words have a creative power. Anytime we speak something, either good or bad, we are giving life to what we are saying. I hear a lot of people going around saying negative things about themselves, their family and their future.

They say things like, "I will never be successful." Or "This sickness is going to get the best of me." Or "Business is so slow I don't think I am going to make it." Or "Flu season is coming, I'll probably get it."
They don't realise they are prophesying their future. The greatest book ever written, the Bible of course, says, "We will eat the fruit of our words," in Proverbs 18:21. That simply means we are going to get exactly what we have been saying.

Here is the key: you've got to send your words out in the direction you want your life to go. You can't speak defeat and expect to have victory. You can't talk about lack and expect to have abundance. You will produce what you've been saying. With your words, you either bless or curse your future.

Learning a new skill

"The more I practise, the luckier I get."
Jerry Barber (1916 – 1994), American professional golfer

To dream is not enough. At some point we have to roll up our sleeves and get down to some serious work; get down to doing everything and anything that is necessary to reach our dreams. This means we need to be daring and ingenious like MacGyver and Houdini, and be a bit of a comedian too, say, like Trevor Noah.

MacGyver (of TV series of the same name) is a fictional top agent for the Phoenix Foundation, a fictional progressive agency devoted to righting the wrongs of the world. He solves complex problems by making use of ordinary objects; he'd rather use a paper clip than a gun to defeat an enemy. Harry Houdini was a real person. Known as the 'Handcuff King', he was probably the world's best and most famous escape artist of all time. He escaped from harrowing situations like being buried alive, thrown into the sea while handcuffed and locked up in a casket. Apparently he could pick a lock with a shoestring.

You can see why I think their skills are useful, can't you? When chasing dreams, it's good to be able to think out of the box and come up with unusual solutions like MacGyver. It's also good to be able to escape, like Houdini, from things and situations that hold us back. And when things go wrong, good people, we need to be like Trevor Noah to see the humour in the situation and laugh even if no one else sees the irony or thinks it's funny. Notwithstanding the useful skills of MacGyver, Houdini and Noah rolled in one, we may need more to make our dreams come true. We may need to develop technical know-how or get an academic qualification or learn soft skills like compassion.

In my experience, learning new skills is part and parcel of the journey towards most dreams. Let me admit that, as an engineer, I thought I knew quite a lot. Isn't that funny? Now I realise I know almost nothing and worst of all, I don't even know what I don't know. I do know, however, that it's important to be aware of the stages of learning or becoming competent.

In psychology, the four stages of competence, or the "conscious competence" learning model, relates to the psychological states involved in the process of progressing from incompetence to competence in a skill.

Competence is the condition of being capable - it is the possession of required skill, knowledge, qualification, or capacity. Initially described as "Four Stages for Learning Any New Skill", the theory was developed at Gordon Training International by its employee Noel Burch in the 1970s. It is now better known as the Hierarchy of Competence and provides a model for learning.

It suggests that individuals are initially unaware of how little they know, or unconscious of their incompetence. As they recognise their incompetence, they consciously acquire a skill, then consciously use it. Eventually, the skill can be utilised without it being consciously thought through: the individual is said to have then acquired 'unconscious' competence.

1. **Unconscious incompetence** - At this level, you are blissfully

ignorant: you have a complete lack of knowledge and skills in a specific area, and you're unaware of this. Your confidence therefore far exceeds your abilities.

You may even deny the usefulness of a skill. Individuals must recognise their own incompetence, and the value of the new skill, before moving on to the next stage. The length of time an individual spends in this stage depends on the strength of the stimulus to learn.

2. Conscious incompetence - By this stage, you've discovered that you need to learn new skills. You realise that others are much more competent than you are, and that they can easily do things that you are struggling with. This level can be demoralising, causing people to lose confidence or even give up on their learning efforts altogether. Therefore, it's important to stay positive at this stage. For me to stay positive and energised to move forward in spite of the challenges, I use affirmations and treasure maps as my tools. I use these two tools to combat negative thinking and to refocus my energy on days when I feel down. Remember, learning might be uncomfortable in the short term, but these skills will help you reach your goals and build a better life. The making of mistakes can be integral to the learning process at this stage.

3. Conscious competence - The individual understands or knows how to do something. However, demonstrating the skill or knowledge requires concentration. It may be broken down into steps, and there is heavy conscious involvement in executing the new skill.

4. Unconscious competence - The individual has had so much practice with a skill that it has become "second nature" and can be performed easily. As a result, the skill can be performed while executing another task. The individual may be able to teach it to others, depending upon how and when it was learned.

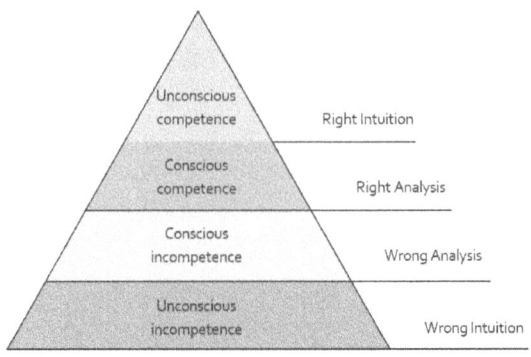

The Hierarchy of Competence by Noel Burch

The Hierarchy of Competence is useful in several ways. First, you can use it to understand the emotions you'll experience during the learning process. This helps you to stay motivated when times get tough; and it helps you manage your expectations of success, so that you don't try to achieve too much, too soon.

For example, during the consciously incompetence phase, you can reassure yourself that, while learning this skill is difficult and frustrating right now, things will improve in the future. And, when you are unconsciously competent, the model reminds you to value the skills you have gained, and not to be too impatient with people who have yet to gain them. It's also useful in coaching and training situations, because it allows you to be in touch with what your people are thinking and feeling. You can help them understand their emotions as they learn new skills, and encourage them when they are feeling disillusioned.

Let me take you through the first tool, namely affirmation, that I have alluded to above. I recommend that you use affirmations to combat negative thoughts as they may derail you if you allow them to take control over you.

Many of us have negative thoughts, sometimes on a regular basis. When we have these thoughts, our confidence, mood and outlook become negative too. The problem with these negative thoughts is that they can be self-fulfilling. Inside our heads, we talk ourselves into believing that we are not good enough. And, because of this, these thoughts drag down our personal lives, our relationships, and our careers. This is why consciously doing the opposite – using positive affirmations – can be helpful. You can use affirmations to drive positive change both in your career and in your life in general.

Affirmations are positive, specific statements that help you to overcome self-sabotaging, negative thoughts. They help you visualise, and believe in, what you are affirming to yourself, helping you to make positive changes to your life and career. Do you remember a time you thought of somebody long enough and out of the blue they called or you bumped into them? It is not a coincidence. It proves that our thoughts have a magnetic power, what you think about, you bring about.

While there's limited research into the effectiveness of using affirmations in a general setting, there's evidence that the use of positive affirmations can successfully treat people with low self-esteem, depression, and other mental health conditions. For instance, in a study by researchers at North Western University, Natchitoches, people who used positive affirmations for two weeks experienced higher self-esteem than at the beginning of the study.

Also, in a study published in the journal of American College Health, researchers found that women treated with cognitive behavioural techniques, which included use of positive affirmations, experienced a decrease in depressive symptoms and negative thinking. A study by researchers at the University of Kentucky, Lexington, had similar results, and came to a similar conclusion.

Of course, it's important to realise that although some people have successfully used affirmations to overcome depression and negative thinking, the technique may not work for everyone. Some people may view affirmations as "wishful thinking," or simply looking at the world with an unrealistic perspective. I must point out it depends on your mindset.

Try looking at positive affirmations this way – many of us do repetitive exercises to improve our body's physical health and condition. Affirmations are like exercises for our mind and outlook; these positive mental repetitions can reprogram our thinking patterns so that, over time, we begin to think, and act, in a new way.

There has also been research that says that the higher your self-esteem, the more effective affirmations can be. This research also found that affirmations can actually have a negative effect if you have low self- esteem. If this applies to you, work on boosting your self-esteem before you use them.

You can use affirmations in any situation where you'd like to see a positive change take place. These might include times when you want to:
- raise your confidence before presentations or important meetings
- control negative feelings such as frustration, anger, or impatience
- improve self-esteem
- finish projects you have started improve your productivity

Affirmations are often more effective when they are paired with other positive thinking and goal-setting techniques. For instance, affirmations work particularly well alongside visualisation. This means that instead of just picturing the change we would like to see with visualisation, we also say it aloud using a positive affirmation.

Affirmations are also useful when setting personal goals. This means once you have identified the goals you would like to achieve in the short- and long-term, you can use positive affirmations to help keep yourself motivated in order to achieve them.

Remember, affirmations are positive statements that help you challenge and overcome negative thinking and self-sabotaging behaviours. They are usually short, positive statements that target a specific area, behaviour,
or belief that you are struggling with. For instance, do you wish you had more patience? Or a deeper relationship with your friends or colleagues? Or do you want a more productive workday?

In closing, let me reiterate that we cannot rely purely on thoughts; we must translate thoughts into words and eventually into actions in order to manifest our intentions. This means we have to be very careful with our words, choosing to speak only those which work towards our benefit and cultivate our highest good. Affirmations help purify our thoughts and restructure the dynamic of our brains so that we truly begin to think nothing is impossible. The word affirmation comes from the Latin *affirmare*, originally meaning "to make steady, strengthen."

Affirmations do indeed strengthen us by helping us believe in the potential of an action we desire to manifest. When we verbally affirm our dreams and ambitions, we are instantly empowered with a deep sense of reassurance that our wishful words will become reality.

Tools & inspiration
Affirmations you can use

"The greatest glory in living lies not in never falling, but rising every time we fall."
Nelson Mandela (1918 – 2013), first democratically elected president of South Africa

When you can't stop comparing yourself to others:
- I have no right to compare myself to anyone for I do not know their whole story.
- I compare myself only to my highest self.
- I choose to see the light that I am to this world.
- I am happy in my own skin and in my own circumstances.
- I see myself as a gift to my people and community and nation.

Affirmations when you get lonely:
- I love and approve of myself.
- I feel the presence of those who aren't physically here.
- I am too big a gift to the world to waste my time on self-pity and sadness.

When you feel you are not good enough no matter how hard you try:

- I am more than good enough and I get better every day.
- I never criticise myself.
- I deserve praise for every bit of progress I make.
- I fully approve of who I am, even as I get better.
- I am a good person at all times of day and night.

I remember Michael Jordan: "I've missed more than 9 000 shots in my career. I've lost almost 300 games, 26 times I've been trusted to take the game winning shot ... and missed. I've failed over and over and over again in my life. That is why I succeed."

When you want to give up:
- I cannot give up until I have tried every conceivable way.
- Giving up is easy and always an option, so let's delay it for another day. I press on because I believe in my path.
- It is always too early to give up on my goals.
- I must know what awaits me at the end of this rope so I do not give up.
- If Thomas Edison had given up, we wouldn't have electric light. He made 1 000 unsuccessful attempts at inventing the light bulb. When a reporter asked, "How did it feel to fail 1 000 times?" Edison replied, "I didn't fail 1 000 times. The light bulb was an invention with 1 000 steps."

When you feel insignificant:
- I am a unique child of this world.
- I have as much brightness to offer the world as the next person.
- I matter and what I have to offer this world also matters.
- I may be one in 7 billion but I am also one in 7 billion.
- Thomas Edison's teachers said he was "too stupid to learn anything". He was fired from his first two jobs for being "non-productive". Albert Einstein was thrown out of school.

Treasure Maps

Close your eyes and imagine yourself where you want to be. You can almost touch it, feel it, smell it, taste it and see it, isn't it? You scan every detail in your mind's eye.

This is a powerful and important technique for motivating yourself and building the self-confidence needed to achieve your goals.

When you open your eyes, the vivid image starts to fade, and it can take real concentration to recreate your visualisation each time you want some inspiration.

What if you could keep hold of that vivid image and refer to it whenever you need a little motivation, or a reminder of what you are working towards? Treasure mapping is a simple tool to help you do just that.

It's a very simple but effective idea: treasure mapping involves creating a physical representation or collage of what you want to achieve. It acts as a constant reminder and representation of your goals. And so it intensifies the effects of visualisation, which acts on your subconscious mind to motivate and encourage you towards achieving those goals.

Let's say you have the ambition to get fitter and run a marathon: Your "treasure map" could include pictures of runners, crossing the marathon finishing line, and athletes training hard; perhaps it could also include pictures of foods that you need to eat (and those you need to avoid). If you are a salesman with the ambition to beat sales records in your company, your treasure map could include a representation of the sales chart you hope to achieve, pictures of people signing deals with customers, pictures of your product standing proud; and perhaps a picture of someone receiving a prize.

The 'worry' factor

"Worry never robs tomorrow of its sorrow; it saps today of its joy."
Leo Buscaglia (1924 – 1998), American author and motivational speaker

I am sure you've heard the story about the man who said he only worries about two things, but here it is anyway: "I only worry about two things – whether I am sick or well. If I'm well, I have nothing to worry about. And if I'm sick, I've only got two things to worry about – whether I get better or whether I die. If I get better, I have nothing to worry about. And if I die, I've only got two things to worry about – whether I go to heaven or hell. If I go to heaven, I have nothing to worry about. And if I go to hell, I'll be so busy greeting my friends I won't have time to worry. So why worry?"
Regardless of how you feel about his view of life after life, he makes a very good point about life. There's really no room for needless concern about the future.

If you're like me, more than once you've found yourself enduring "torments of grief" from evil that has not yet arrived and probably never will. Almost without our being aware of it, healthy concern for the future can be transformed into cancerous worry. We ask ourselves: "What if?", "What if something happens?", "What if things don't turn out?", "What if…?" Worry can become an all-too-constant companion we wish would just go away and leave us alone.

High anxiety about the future doesn't help us with tomorrow's troubles - it only succeeds in ruining today's happiness. The Dalai Lama said something similar. When asked what surprised him most about humanity, he answered, "Man. Because he sacrifices his health in order to make money. Then he sacrifices money to recuperate his health. And then he is so anxious about the future that he does not enjoy the present; the result being that he does not live in the present or the future; he lives as if he is never going to die, and then dies having never really lived."

I believe that needless worry, more than anything else, keeps many people from really living, never mind dreaming! Worry has never helped anyone solve real problems. What is worry other than habitual fear of the future? It is a habit of feeling fear. And, like any other habit, it can be hard to break. But also, like any other habit, it can be replaced with a better one. When you're stuck in life, nothing goes right until you get unstuck. This is a tough one because nobody else but you can get you unstuck from your worries.

There's an urban legend about a man who was thrown into prison and sentenced to death. The night before he was going to be killed, he was given two choices: be shot by a firing squad or open a secret door and escape prison. He thought about his two options. He decided that being shot was going to be less painful and quick, than taking a chance to escape and not knowing what dangers lurked beyond the door. So he was shot and died.

The prison commander was astounded, "He was a good man, who truly believed in his own values and beliefs and I thought he could make a difference in the world, given a second chance. Beyond that door is freedom, I would have turned a blind eye and he would have been a free man."

How many of us are like this prisoner? Plenty, I think. We worry so much about what we don't know. We were indoctrinated to believe ,"better the devil you know than the angel you don't know". Many people are stuck in situations, jobs, relationships, and businesses that are killing them slowly. Yet, because they fear the unknown, they are stuck. They suffer from possibility blindness and arrested development.

Famous motivator Earl Nightingale wrote an article entitled 'The Fog of Worry'. He stated that according to the Bureau of Standards a dense fog covering seven city blocks, to a depth of 100 feet, is composed of something less than one glass of water. So, if all the fog covering seven city blocks, 100 feet deep, were collected and held in a single drinking glass, it would not even fill it. And this could be compared to our worries. If we could see into the future and if we could see our problems in their true light, they wouldn't blind us to the world, to living itself, but could instead be relegated to their true size and place. And if all the things most people worry about were reduced to their true size, you could probably put them all into a drinking glass, too.

Nightingale, in his article which was published in the 2015 book 'The Essence of Success by Earl Nightingale' (the book is a transcript of his over 700 hours of audio programs), further stated that it's a well-established fact that as we get older, we worry less. With the passing of the years and the problems each of them yields, we learn that most of our worries are really not worth bothering ourselves about too much and that we can manage to solve the important ones. But younger people often find their lives obscured by the fog of worry. Yet, here is an authoritative estimate of what of what most people worry about:

- Things that never happen - 40 %. That is, 40 % of the things you worry about will never occur anyway.
- Things over and past that can't be changed by all the worry in the world - 30 %.
- Needless worries about our health - 12 %.
- Petty, miscellaneous worries - 10 %.
- Real, legitimate worries - 8 %. It means 92% of worries is pure fog with no substance at all.

I urge you to write down all the things that concern you and keep you awake at night. Next to each concern or worry you have on the list, write down whether it is something in the past, present or future. If it is in the past, it means that you have no control over it. So stop worrying. It is a waste of your precious time and energy.

If it is something in the present, ask yourself if it is something that you have the power to control or not. If not, avoid thinking about it and instead focus on solving the worries over which you have control.

Let's quickly differentiate between anxiety and worry: anxiety is a feeling of dread, apprehension, uneasiness, shakiness, but often without a specific cause. It produces a sense of approaching danger, but does not always have a reasonable cause.

Worry is a state of being fretful, overly concerned, or anxious expectation. Worry is asking, "What if"? And then answering. Worry is an attempt to move into the future and control it. We pre-image the future. It means "to hang suspended in mid-air".

What causes worry and anxiety? Here are the most common sources:
- Repressed anger
- Unrealistic standards set for us or by us can create anxious tension

- Situations in which a person must make a choice
- Unresolved or undealt-with guilt creates tremendous upheaval
- A lack of faith in ourselves and/or God's purposes

I remember the time when our late president Nelson Mandela was in hospital for a while. People started circulating rumours that if he died, South Africa was going to collapse as a country, there would be war and chaos.

This happened because people couldn't imagine our beautiful country without him. It caused a lot of anxiety and worry among South Africans of all ages and backgrounds. Some people wouldn't even sleep at night thinking about this situation.
When he finally passed on, he was buried and life went ahead without the country getting into a state of chaos. This is the kind of thing that I am talking about.

The mind likes to anchor itself to the known, and the unknown thus creates anxiety. Worry is a symptom of the deeper-rooted fear you experience when you have to tread into the unknown. You prefer things to be predictable.

You fear that any unexpected turn in events would throw your meticulous planning or expectations into disarray. The more energy you give to your fears, the more anxious you become.

In reality, all forms of worry represent an underlying lack of trust. You are unable to trust in the goodness of life. Even though things could turn out in a number of ways, you have a tendency to believe that things are going to turn out negative rather than positive.

Worry displaces. You become ungrounded, with your mind constantly in the future, and find it extremely difficult to be present. You lose the capacity to experience life in the here and now. With worry, you deny yourself the opportunity of living your moments in freedom.

Worrying causes you to leak energy. You feel low. You are more apt to complain about things and compare yourself with others and you're less likely to be rational. Excessive worrying can cause you to stifle your dreams. Your relationships with others get affected, too. No one likes being near a prophet of doom and gloom.

It's important to know that whatever you protect in life, you get to keep. This applies to your worry and your anxiety as well – if you hold to them and protect them, you get to keep them.

Let me hasten to add that it's important to recognise that uncertainty is a natural part of life. You cannot know with absolute certainty what is going to happen next. When you release your attachment to control, it's easier to breathe. Some people deal with anxiety and worry by drinking alcohol,
overeating, doing drugs, and turning to other bad habits. However, none of these are real solutions for worrying. The best approach is to learn how to deal with them in healthy ways.

Tools & inspiration
Dealing with worry and anxiety

"If you are searching for that one person that will change your life, take a look in the mirror."
Unknown

1. Work it off: Although exercise may not actually solve the issues that are causing you to feel anxious, engaging yourself in activity takes your mind off worries. You become clearer after taking a break.

2. Address your fears: Instead of suppressing your anxiety, it is important to face your fears head on. Ask yourself what is truly causing your anxiety. You may even find that your worries are mostly False Evidence Appearing Real.

3. Meditate: Meditation helps your mind with needed breaks from clutter like worries. The practice also helps you achieve greater focus. You find yourself experiencing increased clarity and becoming less likely to worry over unnecessary things.

4. Stay hydrated: Did you know that dehydration has been linked to depression? Just about every person has heard that it is important to drink enough water, but most people do not realise that their mental health actually improves when they are properly hydrated.

5. Change your perspective: Energy flows where you focus your attention. Understand that you can choose to focus on positive rather than negative thoughts. In fact, as you become more positive, you'll be better able to create more positive outcomes.

6. Relax: It's hard not to feel bombarded living in modern times. You probably spend your days in a constant state of flux. Your heart beats a lot faster as a result. So set aside time to relax. You'll find that your feelings of anxiety subside.

7. Seek help: You may find yourself feeling worse and worse if you are unable to stop yourself from incessant worrying. It may be a good idea to seek counselling or to talk to someone who can help. Anxiety is very common. There is nothing to feel ashamed about when you approach someone for help. Some types of anxiety are hereditary; no amount of trying will make them go away, not even my tips above. In such cases, it's best to have a proper assessment done by a qualified psychologist and take the necessary medication available.

8. Let go: The best way to find relief from constant worrying is to let go. Worrying does not bring you any closer to solving problems. In fact, it only makes it more difficult to find clarity.

9. Commit: Make a commitment to reducing your anxiety levels today.

Persistence means keep going

"Many of life's failures are people who did not realise how close they were to success when they gave up."
Thomas Edison (1847 – 1931), American inventor and businessman; invented electric light bulb and the phonograph, amongst other things

Persistence means to be durable, it means lastingness and strength. Persistence breaks resistance. In order to get what you want, you need to get through something. Robert Frost says, "The best way out is always through." What makes people give up on what they started?

Here are some reasons:
- A lack of vision – The Bible says the people perish for the lack of vision
- A wrong belief that life is supposed to be easy
- A wrong belief that success is a final destination
- A lifestyle or habit of giving up
- A lack of resilience

It's important to know first of all that life is not easy. When you are pursuing your goal, you can expect to have a lot of challenges along the way. That is the way life is. There are people who were raised in a protected environment and in a protective way and as a result they are not resilient. All of us are born with an element of resilience, but it needs to be developed like a muscle.

How do you deal with these five enemies of persistence?
- You need to have purpose
- You need to stop making excuses
- You have to develop stamina – to finish what you started

Winston Churchill said, "If you are going through hell, keep going." And Calvin Coolidge said, "Nothing in this world can take the place of persistence. Talent will not: nothing is more common than unsuccessful men with talent. Genius will not; unrewarded genius is almost a proverb. Education will not: the world is full of educated derelicts. Persistence and determination alone are omnipotent." So you have to press on and keep on pressing on.

Know that no amount of planning, action and goal-setting can predict the unpredictable. Often you will need to persist in the face of adversity.

In order to persist, you need inward strength and this inward strength can only be found in the relationship you have with God, for He is the strength. Additional strength can also be found in the relationships you have, so it's important to team up with the right people. This means that when your watch is broken, don't take it to the mechanic, take it to the jeweller. Get the right help and just press on and keep on pressing on.

Talking about quitting, a few people come to mind; people that didn't quit when faced with adversity: Nelson Mandela, Steve Biko, Robert Sobukwe, Dr Martin Luther King Jnr, Mahatma Gandhi, Michael Jordan, and so on and so forth.

Why did Nelson Mandela prefer imprisonment for 27 years when he had the option to be free? Why would Michael Jordan continue playing basketball after being cut from his high school team and being told he was not good enough? Why would Oprah Winfrey continue with her television career after she was fired from her television reporting job as she was deemed "not suitable for television"? These names I have just mentioned rose to be great figures in the world in their respective fields and the mere mention of these names brings a smile to our faces; they represent tenacity, strength, persistence, conviction and mastery.

I am sure there's something that you are working on that has been or is being rejected. Don't give up; think instead of these names and always be reminded that it is always too soon to quit.
Henry Ford said, "Failure gives you the opportunity to begin again more intelligently." I have failed a number of times myself, and I hate it, but I always win in my failure, that is my outlook on life.

Sadly, most people are where they are because of the influence of the people before them. You may be an engineer because you were talked into it or because your father or brother was one. You are running a restaurant simply because that's what your family did for years and it became a natural thing for you to do, not because it's something you love doing. Many people are into jobs they hate. They can't wait for lunch time, to knock off in the afternoon and are always looking forward to Fridays. This is living a life of running away from your dream.
The workplace is supposed to be a platform for you to shine brighter, but instead most people see the workplace as a horrible place, a prison of sorts. Most people think a prison is about physical walls; to me it's more about your thoughts that are locked while your body is free. Your prayers should include revelation, asking God to show you that one thing that will lead to fulfilment and happiness. Knowing what you want is embedded deep down in you, it's not out there. You just need something, a stimuli that will ignite your dream. So be open to experiences as you don't know which stimuli will do the trick.

Tools & inspiration
Developing persistence

"Your persistence is your measure of faith in yourself."
Unknown

Three things that you need to develop persistence:
A. Revelation – a revelation that your life is supposed to be fantastic. This revelation is the illumination, it is the knowing that God has a great plan for your life. There's a good idea and a God idea. A good idea may come to pass, but God's idea must come to pass.

B. Conviction – feeling and knowing that this is going to work. So a revelation leads to conviction. When you know that something will work because you have a clear picture of it, no one can stop you from pursuing it.

C. Movement – this is the action you take to make your revelation a reality. This is when you put plans in place and start executing them.

I saw myself standing in front of a thousand people motivating them. This was my revelation and it lead to conviction, that knowing that this was going to work no matter what. I started reading more, got mentorship, started writing articles that ended up being noticed by the local newspaper and published as columns. This all happened because of the three things above. There were so many difficult moments, but I stayed the course and pressed on. Once again I proved that persistence breaks resistance. Today I speak for corporates and am living a purposeful life.

The four life changing Ds

When I look back at my life all I can see is the four Ds that positively turned my life around and can surely change yours too. Let me share them with you:

1. Disgust - One Friday evening in May 2011, I took my family out for movies and dinner. When we were 10 minutes into the movie, I received a call from work, which was about a machine breakdown. I had to go to work because as head of engineering, I had to make a serious decision. I missed out on quality time with my family. When I came back two and half hours later, their dinner appetite had gone down the tube and they were waiting for me in the freezing cold outside. I was so disgusted by this, as it had happened a few times before. This time I said, "Enough is enough; I have had it; I am sick and tired of being sick and tired."

2. Decision - I took a decision that I was never going to let my family down again in that way. I resigned a week later; that was my way out. This step was about taking action, not talking and breaking promises anymore. I had done it enough times already.

3. Desire - I so wanted to start my own business, but didn't have courage. One thing about desire is that it waits for the trigger, something to happen. That thing can be a song, movie, talk with someone, anger, seminar, fight, sermon, sight of a baby crawling, anything! So, always welcome all experiences in life as they carry the potential to change life. The trick is that you will never know which trigger or event will turn everything upside down. Don't put walls around you because you will deprive yourself of opportunities out there.

4. Determination - This is promising yourself you will never give up. Nothing can resist a human will. This is saying I will do it or die. This is doing whatever it takes (legally of course) to get what you want.

I have since shed many tears, lost some friends, felt deserted by my own family at times, spent sleepless nights, been ridiculed, had an empty bank account and so on, as a result of my decision. You see, this is what I mean by resolve, not giving up on your dream. If I gave up, you wouldn't be reading these words. I trust these four Ds will help you change your life.

Be careful what you wish for

"Freedom is not the right to live as you please, but the right to find how we ought to live in order to fulfill our potential."

Ralph Waldo Emerson(1803 – 1882), American essayist, lecturer and poet

I am fortunate to have personally known a lottery winner. He was a teacher who lived an average life and drove an average car, a Toyota Corolla.

He won R4-million rand in the lottery. His dream came true. He immediately quit his job, bought himself a top of the range car, gold in colour. He sold his old house in a township and bought one in the northern suburbs. He started acquiring a few businesses as part of investing his money. To him this was going to last forever. He had no business experience. Teaching kids was all he had done in his life. Things started to spiral out of control as he started drinking whisky every day and surrounded himself with new friends. He thought he was living the good life.

He started coming back home from his meetings at 2am, 3am, 5am and some days never came back. He was the man of the moment, while abusing his family. He bought entertainment from young girls and, horror of horrors, even took them home with him.

His businesses soon collapsed. The money soon disappeared and he fell sick as a result of stress. All his acquired 'friends' and entertainers vanished. His family was exposed to abuse and embarrassment. His lungs failed him and he died four years later.

I often hear people saying I will be so happy if I win the lottery, get a rich partner, get another job and so on and so forth. The question is – are you mentally, emotionally, spiritually and even physically ready for what you wish for? Be careful what you wish and ask for. Be careful what you dream of. Please don't be caught up in a similar situation as above. Ask yourself today what you will do if you were to get that amount of money and then write the answers down. Your dream should be something that enriches you far beyond money; something that will make this world a much better place than how you found it.

Money does not mean success. Success starts with a prepared mind. So, invest in your mind, it is the best investment you can ever make. It all starts with the correct philosophy, or mind-set.

One question I normally ask people who come for my coaching sessions is, "Imagine your kids were to come running to you to tell you that when they grow up they want to be exactly like you. Would you be happy and proud of them?" Almost all the people I have asked this question said "No." On asking why they wouldn't be happy, they said they wouldn't like their kids to repeat the same errors in judgement.

It is crystal clear that people know they are not doing their best, they have settled for less. Some blame the system, politics, weather, taxes, parents and even their dogs, for not achieving their dreams. Instead of blaming, I

recommend thinking very carefully about what you wish for in the first place and in the second place, tapping into your resourcefulness or creativity – the real lottery which is inside you.

Don't hesitate to dedicate long hours to developing your creativity and your ability to achieve your dream.

This is where you have to make time for important matters, and cut out the busyness in your life which doesn't yield any positive results in your life. Sydney Howard said, "One half of knowing what you want, is knowing what you are willing to give up before you get it."

Give up bad habits and time-wasters like wishing you won the lottery! One thing I have learnt is that there is nothing as pricey as a regret - a regret of time wasted, energy wasted, potential wasted, and missed opportunities and relationships. All the action is in the here and now and once missed,

it is gone forever. I have learnt to take my chances and pursue my dreams no matter the cost as it will never, ever come close to the cost of regretting what could, should, would have been done. You only regret the past and what was not done, never the present or future, that's how life is. So, listen to that inner voice and pursue your dreams.

When I needed a bakkie to remove building rubble from my house, I was referred to a very humble gentleman who owned one and was in the business of rubble removal. While his assistant was busy loading the rubble, I asked him how he got into that business. He said he had previously worked for a projects company and that he and his colleagues were transported

to a project site every morning and back in the evening. This happened for about seven years. In summer it would be hot at the back of the bakkie and some days it rained and everyone got soaking wet. In winter it was ice cold and windy. One cold day, on the way back from a site, the gentleman got off from the bakkie and said to himself, "I will never be rained on and be so cold like this ever again."

Today he has four bakkies and he is doing well. You will never know if you are able to pick something up until you attempt to pick it up. He tried something instead of wishing for a lottery win. He bought bakkies, not lottery tickets. His former colleagues are still stuck in their jobs.

Maybe you are in a situation or a relationship that is not ideal. Let your frustration work for you, let it bring out the best in you. Say, 'I am sick of this, I am tired of being treated like this and I am going to reach for my dreams, going to go for the awesome life that I have been wanting to have!"

If you won the lottery and got enough money to last for the rest of your life, would you continue doing what you are doing right now? Would you really wake up on a Monday with a big smile on your face? If the answer is 'yes', then you are in the right place but if it's 'no', then you have to find that thing that you would be able to look forward to do on a Monday morning with a big smile.

Tools & inspiration
Look beyond the obvious

There is no man who isn't capable of doing more than he thinks he can do."
Henry Ford (1863 – 1947), founder of the Ford Motor Company

The most important thing to do in order to achieve your goals, is to develop the right behaviour by improving the quality of your questions. Stating the obvious is saying, "I don't have the key to open the door." The question should rather be, "How can I open the door without the key?" Sadly, most people get lost or stuck in the obvious and give up looking for possible solutions. Escape artist Houdini opened locks with shoestrings and burglars find all kinds of tools to open doors and break in, so surely there must be more than one way to open a door without a key.

Write down one thing that can make a positive difference in your life. Your intention with this exercise is to create a new behaviour, not a once-off feat. This one thing must be able to stretch you.

It is who you become through the process that matters most, rather than the results achieved.

Goal-setting questions:

1. Why is it important to me? Generate at least 5 reasons.
2. How can I achieve it? Don't try to qualify your answers. Just write down whatever idea comes to mind. Generate at least ten different ways.
3. Who can help me achieve it? Think of people you know and those you don't know but wish you knew.
4. When do I want to complete it? Pick a date, month and a year.

5. The last step is to ask yourself the following question. If I want to achieve this thing by the date stated in step 4, which option of the ones stated in step 2 will be most appropriate to ensure positive results, and so it goes on.

Avoid these time-wasters

- Too much sleeping
- Too much TV watching
- Too much gaming
- Too much day dreaming without a concrete plan
- Too much shopping
- Socialising with negative friends that are always complaining and blaming everything on the planet, and/or friends that nurse your ego, telling you what you want to hear not what you need to hear.

Dealing with fear and risk

"You learn how to cut down trees by cutting them down."
Traditional proverb of the Central African Bateke people

I truly believe that all of us are given gifts, talents and abilities to share with the world. If you do not use what has been given to you, your life will be full of gaps and empty holes and you will have no happiness and peace in your life.

Sadly, some people try to fill these holes with things like drugs, alcohol, watch too much TV, spending time surfing on the Internet, playing games on a mobile phone, hanging around with like-minded people complaining about the world and its people, and worrying.

When you don't have a true appreciation and acceptance for who you are, you will allow yourself to be held captive by fear and to be immobilised by it. In the process, you begin to abuse yourself, sabotage your dreams and unconsciously work against yourself, becoming your own worst enemy.

I have discovered it myself and have also learned from numerous studies, that failure to take risks by allowing fear to keep you captive, leads to a miserable life. It is for this reason that I have chosen to write again on fear and risk. I touched a bit on these two subjects in my previous book, 'You Are Born to Win', but I feel I need to add more meat because of the seriousness of these two four-letter words.

Let me start off with fear. According to Dr Ari Brown, MD, co-author of Baby 411 (Windsor Peak Press), human beings are born with two fears: loud noises and falling. "Babies' brains and nerves grow rapidly in the first two years of life, but they are born with very immature nervous systems," says Dr. Brown. "This means that they cannot interpret or handle certain sensory input - like loud noises or the feeling of falling." That's why passing an infant around to loving relatives may not bother your baby, but set him down too fast or make an abrupt, loud noise, and he'll cry in fright.

Studies have revealed that fear is a number one killer of dreams. Fear is the subtlest and most destructive of all human diseases. Fear kills dreams, hope and can hold you back from doing that which you are capable of doing. Let me hasten to indicate that there's legitimate (or good) fear and bad fear. It is bad fear that is a killer of dreams.

Let me share an example of good or legitimate fear: I had a friend Mike, who passed away some years ago. He was overweight and I said to him why don't you come and join me at the gym and lose some weight? He told me he had tried to lose weight, but was convinced that he couldn't lose it because he was big boned. I am sure you have heard this before from someone. To be honest with you, I have never seen a fat skeleton, have you? Anyway, he was totally sold on this fallacy that he couldn't lose weight. One day he fell sick and collapsed at work and was rushed to hospital. The doctor examined him and after doing blood tests, he told him that he was diabetic. The doctor said he had to change his lifestyle, especially his eating habits. The doctor further told him about the side effects of his condition: lack of concentration, high blood pressure, unconsciousness, poor vision, heart diseases, and impotence. All along, Mike remained quiet, listening.

"What have you just said, Doctor?" The Doctor repeated, "Yes, you will become impotent."

This one word changed his whole life. He started jogging every day and changed his eating habits. I am convinced that without this word he would have continued with his old eating habits. He changed his lifestyle and in time he was in good shape.

So, this is an example of good fear, it motivates or pushes you to act as a matter of urgency and do whatever possible to change.

So, what do you need to change? Don't leave it until it's too late. Are you waiting for a doctor to tell you must change or that you are about to die?

The first step to confronting your fear is to realise and acknowledge that you have gifts, talents and abilities given to you by God at birth. And that without living them, your life won't count for anything, it will be empty and painful. This realisation and acknowledgement will create power, that special drive within you that will push you through your fear. The truth is that whatever you resist, will persist. So you need to take a step forward. That step is to imagine yourself being more than able and capable of handling your fears. This involves writing down what you stand to gain if you didn't have fear.

The next step is to learn to accept fear as a 'fact not a force' to block you from achieving your dreams. Fear has no force except the one you give it. Just accept the fact that you are afraid and move on anyway. Watch your inner conversation, discipline your thinking and imagination because if you don't, your mind will take you on a wild trip.

Whenever you hear your lower-self talking to you about what you can't do, it's time to stand up to it and talk to yourself. Be your own motivator, build yourself by seriously talking to yourself affirming how great you are. You really have to stand up inside yourself. The world and people around you may be putting or pushing you down, but if you are standing up inside yourself, you will eventually conquer, you will emerge victorious.

You either have fear or fear has you!

When you face your fears, you realise that it's not as bad as you think or as people said it is. You will begin to see fear as a fact, not a force. A few years ago when I told my family and friends I was done with the corporate career and was starting my own business, there was much wailing and gnashing of teeth.

They told me I had made a bad decision, and even worse, it was during the economic downturn. I was told my decision was illogical and also that there were many companies that were doing what I was going to do and they were closing down. I, however, made the decision to follow my heart.

Today, with a successful business, I am happy and confronting new challenges. I always wanted to write a book. When I spoke to people about this they were sceptical. Some had tried, but not finished. Publishers are difficult to find if you are not a well-known author. It's difficult to write, and sometimes your ideas and inspiration dries up.

And all these things are true. It took a long time. I ended publishing myself. And there were some days that I felt like giving up, it was tough. I stood inside myself when the world around me was pushing me down and doubting my abilities. I fought for what I envisaged for myself.

On my birthday, February 22, 2015, I successfully launched my first book, 'You Are Born to Win'. I then wanted to host my own seminars. I was told that I was not a big or known brand and that I was just courting failure and heartache. Yes, it was tough and I had limited resources, but I became resourceful and pushed forward. On November 14, 2015, the 'Get Inspired Seminar' was held at Emperors Palace, east of Johannesburg. I am sharing this information with you to show you that, I have had a fair share of challenges in my life and am still having them, but I face them head on. As long as you stand inside yourself when the world doubts you and you continue fighting for what your heart desires, you will emerge victorious.

Nobody has the power to stop a resolute mind.

As you work on yourself to discover your true identity, you will discover that you have lots of power lying dormant inside of you.

I am reminded of a story I once heard about a man who was doing special research on a tribe of head hunters (headhunting is the practice of taking and preserving a person's head after killing the person). He had difficulty in developing a relationship and rapport with the tribesmen because he feared them. For a long time, he was imprisoned by fear. Finally, one night while he was in bed, he said to himself, "Research is what I came here to do and I know that there's a risk involved and I am going to do it, come what may. I am not going to be afraid anymore."

He went back the next day and started to do his work, interviewing members of the tribe and they began to respond to him. People were surprised by his results and asked how he managed to get close to such hostile tribesmen to get the valuable information. His answer, that I think is of value to all of us, was, "When life can no longer threaten you with death, what else is there?"

The truth is that the majority of our fears are not about life and death. We blow things out of proportion giving fears the power they don't have or deserve and we allow them to control and govern our lives. Most of the time we allow ourselves to be programmed into thinking we are not worthy of our dreams and aspirations. Reading newspapers and watching all kinds of news on television and listening to the news on radio can make you afraid to come out of the house. So, what kind of thoughts are you feeding your mind every day? Mahatma Gandhi said, "I will not let anyone walk through my mind with their dirty feet." And Jim Rohn further said, "Every day, stand guard at the door of your mind." Be careful of the thoughts you are feeding your consciousness. You can either use fear as a blocker or as a building block. Instead of feeling powerless you can feel powerful.

When you feel positive about yourself and you truly feel that you deserve something, you will go after whatever you want with power and purpose no matter what. You will become unstoppable. It is this feeling and thinking that will give you the power to create what you deserve. This will create a will and the truth is that where there's a will, there is a way.

Just take a moment and think about how your life and future would be if you didn't allow fear to have its way with you...If you have been imprisoned by fear, now is the time to break the bondage. Say, " I feel the fear, but I will do this anyway." Is it easy? No. Can you do it? Yes.

To get started on the journey to your dream, you may need someone to hold on to, someone who is more courageous or has more experience. Be willing to reach out in order to get some assistance. Remember that only the weak are afraid to ask for help.

Expect and deal with CRAP (criticism, rejection, adversity and prejudice).

Don't do things you don't want to do just because you fear being disliked or criticised by others. Bill Cosby said, "I don't know the key to success, but the key to failure is trying to please everybody." This is not the kind of world where you will be liked by everybody, just accept that. You are the star of your show, refuse to be the extra in your own movie.

"Before you are boxed and buried, decide now you will box and bury your fears," says Les Brown "Growth is painful; Change is painful. But nothing is as painful as staying stuck somewhere you don't belong," says Mandy Hale.

Ask yourself, "What chances do I need to take? What risks do I need to embrace? What fears do I need to step on?" In life you either live your dreams or your fears - it's your choice, choose wisely.

Now let's take a look at risk. Dr David Viscot, the author of the book entitled 'Risking' wrote, "If you cannot risk, you cannot grow; if you cannot grow, you cannot become your best. If you cannot become your best, you cannot be happy. If you cannot be happy, what else is there?" Let me unwrap the statement in a step-by-step formula that will make it easier for you to follow and understand:

Risk = Growth

If you cannot risk, you cannot grow. Here Dr Viscot suggests that in order to grow you must take some risk. There are different types of areas we can grow in: mental, physical, emotional, and spiritual.

Dr Erik Erikson, the famous psychologist (1902-1994) who proposed that we all go through eight stages of growth, found that unresolved childhood developmental tasks "leave a life-long residue of emotional immaturity." The growth stages are generally infant, child, youth, adolescence, teen, young adults, adults, and elders. Even though there are ages assigned to these stages, everyone is different and some people can appear to stay younger longer than others. However, we have to go through these stages eventually or die trying:

- Mentally, in order to grow, we must challenge our current frame of thought and be open (risk) to new ideas, methodologies, and thoughts. If we were to keep the basic same beliefs and knowledge we would never learn or grow.

- Physically, this growth happens when we push our bodies past what the body considers "normal." Let's consider your bicep. In order for it to grow, we must add more weight over time. If you continually lift the same amount of weight, you will eventually reach a point where your muscle will no longer grow. By lifting more and more weight, you risk injury and overuse. Therefore, it is the safe, right amount of risk that manages healthy growth.

- Emotionally, the capacity to be aware of, control, and express one's emotions, and to handle interpersonal relationships judiciously and empathetically. Emotional development also goes through stages, and if we are healthy the emotional development matches physical development. I believe that we go through the emotional stages of helplessness and need, formation of personality, fear and suffering, responsibility and acceptance, and finally, peace.

- Spiritually, growth comes from a better understanding of ourselves and the world around us. When we allow new beliefs to enter our mind, we have to again risk being wrong or challenging our past understanding. Spiritual growth only comes from letting down the defences of our mind and allowing in new beliefs and understandings.

Growth = Becoming Your Best

If you cannot grow you cannot become your best. What does becoming your best mean to you? To me, it is realising true potential. Potential is defined

as the capacity to become something bigger and better in the future and is different for everyone. I truly believe we can all achieve great things. All of us have different unique abilities to be our best, with one constant, universal refrain: you will never reach your true potential if your skill-set and mind-set do not grow.

Similar to risk, you must be willing to learn, adapt, and change in order to grow. It is those changes to our mind-set that allow us to realise our true potential. One could almost jump straight from risk to potential, but growth is needed because as we realise our best, we learn paths to take and which ones to avoid. So, growth allows us to learn and build upon that learning, thus realising our best.

Best = Happiness

If you cannot become your best, you cannot be happy. When you talk to those around you who are truly happy, are they people who are satisfied with their lives or do they constantly want more without actively working towards it? I find that those who are truly happy are the ones who feel they are living life on their own terms. They are happy because they are fulfilled.

When I see people fulfilled, I see them at their best. Happiness is finding joy in the life you live. If your life is not as you want it, you are not operating at your true potential. I see this all the time in people's jobs. People take a job or enter into a relationship for wrong reasons or because they think they have to. They don't feel fulfilled. The lack of fulfilment leads to underperformance and unhappiness. Conversely, people who seem to be exceedingly happy, are those that work to their true potential, becoming their best.

Happiness = Purpose

If you cannot be happy, what else matters? Happiness, for me, is about finding purpose and following my dreams. Life is not a dress rehearsal; you've got

one life to live to the fullest. Many people are miserable and unhappy with who they are, what they have become, and what their prospects are for life. They live life like someday it will be different, they sit and wait. I have learned that life doesn't change, you must change your life through your actions and decisions. If you really want to be happy you have to make it. You cannot 'find' happiness, you must create happiness. Studies have revealed that over 40% of the things we worry about never come to pass. It is this worry of nothing that leads to fear, which is the acronym of False Expectation Appearing Real. Fear can be used to our advantage. I want you to imagine how your life would be

if you didn't allow fear to have you by the scruff of your neck. You are blessed with gifts, talents, abilities, and power to dream far beyond any other creature in the world. You can, without hesitation, crush your fears, take risks and reach for your dream.

Tools & inspiration
The night conversation

"Everybody is a genius. But if you judge a fish by its ability to climb a tree, it will live its whole life believing that it is stupid."
Albert Einstein (1879 – 1955), theoretical physicist

Imagine this:
As you pull the blanket and are about to switch off the bed-side lamp and sleep after a hard day's work, you hear a knock on your bedroom's door and a towering figure moves in slowly towards you.

While you are still surprised and confused at what is happening, the voice from this huge figure says: "I am your maker and am here to take you home with me. I have given you so many years (whatever your age) and all you needed to do, was to be the best you. But instead, you chose to be like everybody else. You have settled for so little when I have given you so much and so many possibilities."
He further says, "I give you one minute to give me a reason why I must not take you home with me tonight, why do you deserve tomorrow?"

You: I'll stop wasting precious time complaining, blaming, and criticising everybody and everything for my incompetence and shortcomings. I give you my word, please trust me.
Maker: "I trusted you since day one, but you have given nothing except empty promises. Show me your goals, let me see."
You: I don't have them in writing.
Maker: "You have been told so many times to write down your goals. Your life is just full of empty promises and unfulfilled dreams and I cannot allow you to

continue living like this anymore. You have wished and kept your fingers crossed that one day things will change for the better, but you have never taken any action and are simply wasting time and wasting life. Come with me, let's go, your place is needed for someone else."

Cheers to your success

"We face neither East nor West: we face forward."
Kwame Nkrumah (1909 – 1972), Africa's first black prime minister

The moment you see successful people as an example of what is possible for you rather than an exception, is the moment you embark on your own success.

As a professional speaker, author and life coach, I am often asked what success is. I get totally excited when I start thinking, or speaking or writing about success. I see success everywhere. Small successes, big successes. Success means different things to different people, but in my humble opinion, success is about self-expression. It's about becoming the best you, and doing that which gladdens your heart in a way you cannot describe.

"Success is a progressive realisation of a worthy ideal," said Earl Nightingale. So if you are a plumber, teacher, petrol attendant, sweeper, nurse or whatever because you always wanted be one and you are doing it well, then you are successful. My purpose in life is to inspire people to realise their potential and achieve their dreams. I regard myself as successful, because I wanted to do this and am now doing it.

Success to me is not just about the accumulation of materialistic things, but being the best that you can be and this can only be if you do what you always wanted to do. If you are conforming to other people's expectations of you, then who will be the real you?

What causes you to become as excited as a kid in a candy store? What is it that you never tire of doing, that you never say it's Friday afternoon or Sunday, that it's too cold or too hot, that you'll sacrifice your television time, your friends and your sleep for? Success is being able to do this thing that you so much enjoy!

Success is about being the person you dreamed of becoming. It's not about leading the pack or coming first in the race of life, but leading yourself well. Life is about running your own race, it's about being the best person you can ever be. It's a peace of mind attained only through self-satisfaction in knowing you made the effort to do the best you are capable of.

Success requires one to have a 'personal' goal, dream, vision and a purpose. Your purpose in life is the reason for your existence, the reason you were born. As a human-being, you are born with dignity, you are worthy, your life counts and your life has ultimate significance. You were born for a reason. God created you the way you are for a particular reason and purpose. Never allow yourself to feel inferior because of your biological features; that's how God wanted you to be. Focus on what matters most, your life's purpose, and not what people say about you.

It therefore doesn't matter who you are, irrespective of your skin colour, education, social standing and family background, you are a human-being before anything else and you are not less than anyone in the world. This should be your life's driving principle. God created all of us equal and all the inequalities are therefore man-made. Once you understand this, peace will be with you forever. The truth is that you have gifts, talents, potential and abilities nobody has in the world. You are unique and special. The sooner you realise and embrace this truth the better it will be for you. Winston Churchill said, "The truth is incontrovertible, malice may attack it; ignorance may deride; but in the end, there it is." You cannot run away from the truth, you can only embrace it and it will then set you free!

For me, success is about upgrading; about becoming more and better than you were previously. It's about climbing to the next level. Nelson Mandela explained that once you reach the top of the mountain, you realise that there are many other mountains to climb. Why limit yourself to only one mountain?

I also love what Jim Rohn said, "When the end comes for you, let it find you conquering a new mountain, not sliding down an old one." Not getting stuck in one mountain complaining about what could have been, is success. Never stop growing or dreaming.

Making things happen, is success. Conquering your fears is success. Feeling happy and content is success. Reading this book – or any worthwhile book – from beginning to end is success.
Being the real you is success. Cheers to your success!

Tools & inspiration
The night conversation

"Your time is limited, so don't waste it living someone else's life."
Steve Jobs (1955 – 2011), American information technology entrepreneur and inventor; co-founder, chairman, and chief executive officer of Apple Inc.

Is engineering a tough and complex field reserved for only the brightest minds? I don't think so. I believe that everyone can benefit from applying basic engineering principles to everyday life. This can be done step-by-step in an easy to follow manner.

Let me share with you the four vital steps that will help you engineer your way to success:

1. Structure
To get started – no matter what goal you want to achieve – you need to put structures in place. This means creating a framework that will carry your dream forward and includes: a physical framework (place); emotional framework (support group like family and friends); financial framework (access to money) and strategic framework (like a business plan).

2. System
Then you need to get a system going. This means you need to find a way of bringing all the different practical elements together and make them work and yield results.

3. Maintenance

You need to take care of the structure and system to sustain your success. Most known failures are as a result of neglecting maintenance. This applies to your body, car, relationship, business and everything else. Maintenance means paying attention to detail on an ongoing basis. It's hard and dirty work, hence it is often neglected and results in major failures. Have you heard of loadshedding? That came about mainly due to a lack of maintenance to electricity infrastructures such as power stations.

4. Innovation

The world is changing at lightning speed and one must keep up to date. Ask yourself two critical questions:

a. How else can I do this? In other words, is there a better way of doing what I am doing? Engineers and entrepreneurs are always looking for new ways of doing things. Copy them!
b. What else can I do? Is there anything else that I can do in addition to what I am already doing?

These key questions will help you generate new ideas continuously and remain relevant, productive, effective and efficient.

Engineering 'thinking' has definitely helped me and I invite you to give it a try as well.

Start applying the structure-system-maintenance-innovation principles as soon as you can in your life and see the difference. It goes without saying that you need to believe that you can do it.

How to find your life's purpose

"Feeling sorry for yourself, and your present condition, is not only a waste of energy but the worst habit you could possibly have."

Dale Carnegie (1888 – 1955), author of bestseller book 'How to win friends and influence people'

Among the feedback I receive from my talks, life coaching sessions and weekly articles, I often hear the comment, "I just don't know what I want, I can't figure out what I want to do."

I find this fascinating – that so many people have lost touch with who and what they want to be professionally. I realise that we like to blame the economy and our money problems for our unhappiness, but that's not the root cause of this career malaise. There are other reasons for feeling

disconnected from what you do for a living. Who would have believed that there could be millions of people working in jobs and careers they hate, not able to figure out how they want to be of service in the world?

I think that people make rigid assumptions about what they need to be happy or what they're capable of creating. These assumptions (often unconscious) keep them trapped in a tight little box with a lid that won't budge.

Some of these limiting assumptions are:

- I need to earn Rx to live the life I want
- My marriage or family won't survive my making this change
- I'll be too old by the time I make this change
- I don't have what it takes to reinvent myself or even repurpose what I do
- I'm a loser and a failure – I can't compete
- I'm too unskilled or out of touch with current trends
- I have nothing important to offer
- I'm not special
- I'm too beat up and burnt out
- Nothing else will be better

We have no idea what we want to do with our lives. Even after we finish school. Even after we get a job. Even after we're making money. I changed career aspirations myself. And even after I had a business, it wasn't until a few years later that I clearly defined what I wanted for my life.

Chances are you're like I was and have no clue what you want to do. It's a struggle almost every adult goes through. "What do I want to do with my life?", "What am I passionate about?", "What do I not suck at?"

I receive emails from people in their 40s, 50s and even 60s who still have no clue what they want to do with themselves.

Here's the truth. We exist on this earth for some undetermined period of time. During that time we do things. Some of these things are important. Some of them are unimportant. And those important things give our lives meaning and happiness. The unimportant ones basically just kill time.

So when people say, "What should I do with my life?" or "What is my life purpose?" what they're actually asking is, "What can I do with my time that is important?"

This is an infinitely better question to ask. It's far more manageable and it doesn't have all of the ridiculous baggage that the 'life purpose' question does. There's no reason for you to be asking these important questions of your life while sitting on your couch all day watching TV. Rather, you should be doing something and discovering what feels important to you.

What is your legacy going to be? What are the stories people are going to tell when you're gone? What is your obituary going to say? Is there anything to say at all? If not, what would you like it to say? How can you start working towards that, today?

When people feel like they have no sense of direction, no purpose in their life, it's because they don't know what's important to them, and they don't know what their values are.

And when you don't know what your values are, then you're essentially taking on other people's values and living other people's priorities instead of your own. This is a one-way ticket to unhealthy relationships and eventual misery.

Discovering one's purpose in life essentially boils down to finding those one or two things that are bigger than yourself, and bigger than those around you. And to find them you must get off your couch and act.

What do I want to do with my life? It's a question all of us think about at one point or another. For some, the answer comes easily. For others, it takes a lifetime to figure out. It's easy to just go through the motions and continue to do what's comfortable and familiar. But for those of you who seek fulfilment, who want to do more, these questions will help you paint a clearer picture of what to do with your life.

1. What are the things I'm most passionate about?

The first step to living a more fulfilling life is to think about the things that you're passionate about. What do you love? What fulfils you? What "work" do you do that doesn't feel like work? Maybe you enjoy writing, maybe you love working with animals or maybe you have a knack for photography.

The point is, figure out what you love doing, then do more of it.

2. What are my greatest accomplishments in life so far?

Think about your past experiences and the things in your life you're proudest of. How did those accomplishments make you feel? Pretty darn good, right? So why not try and emulate those experiences and feelings? If you ran a marathon once and loved the feeling you had afterwards, start training for another one. If your child grew up to be a star athlete or musician because of your teachings, then be a coach or mentor for other kids. Continue to do the things that have been most fulfilling for you.

3. If my life had absolutely no limits, what would I choose to have and what would I choose to do?

Here's a cool exercise: think about what you would do if you had no limits. If you had all the money and time in the world, where would you go? What would you do? Who would you spend time with?

These answers can help you figure out what you want to do with your life. It doesn't mean you need millions of rands to be happy though. What it does mean is answering these questions will help you set goals to reach certain milestones and create a path toward happiness and fulfilment.

4. What are my goals in life?
Goals are a necessary component to set you up for a happy future. So answer these questions:
What are your health goals? What are your career goals? What are your family goals? Once you figure out the answers to each of these, you'll have a much better idea of what you should do with your life.

5. Whom do I admire most in the world?
Following the path of successful people can set you up for success. Think about the people you respect and admire most. What are their best qualities? Why do you respect them? What can you learn from them?
It's been said that you're the average of the five people you spend the most time with. So don't waste your time with people who hold you back from achieving your dreams. Spend more time with happy, successful, optimistic people and you'll become one of them.

6. What do I not like to do?
An important part of figuring out what you want to do with your life is honestly assessing what you don't want to do. What are the things you despise? What bugs you the most about your current job? Maybe you hate meetings even though you sit through six hours of them every day. If that's the case, find a job where you can work more independently. The point is, if you want something to change in your life, you need to take action.

7. How hard am I willing to work to get what I want?
Great accomplishments never come easy. If you want to do great things with your life, you're going to have to make a great effort. That will probably mean putting in more hours than the average person, getting outside your comfort zone and learning as much

as you can.

But here's the cool part: it's often the journey that is the most fulfilling part. It's during these seemingly small, insignificant moments that you'll often find 'aha' moments that help you answer the question, "What do I want to do with my life?"

So take the first step toward improving your life. You won't regret it.

8. What is true about you today that would make your 8-year-old self cry?

When I was a child, I used to write stories and enjoy poetry. I used to sit for hours by myself, writing away, and reading some books and newspapers. Not because I wanted anyone to read it. Not because I wanted to impress my parents or teachers. But for the sheer joy of it. And then, for some reason, I stopped. And I don't remember why. We all have a tendency to lose touch with what we loved as children. Something about the social pressures of adolescence and professional pressures of young adulthood squeezes the passion out of us. We're taught that the only reason to do something is if we're somehow rewarded for it.

It wasn't until I was in my mid-20s that I rediscovered how much I loved writing. And it wasn't until I started my business that I remembered how much I enjoyed writing, motivating and inspiring others - something I did in my early teens, just for fun.

The funny thing though, is that if my 8-year-old self had asked my 20-year- old self, "Why don't you write anymore?" and I replied, "Because I'm not good at it," or "Because nobody would read what I write," or "Because you can't make money doing that," not only would I have been completely wrong, but that 8-year-old boy version of myself would have probably started crying.

9. What makes you forget to eat and visit friends?

We've all had that experience where we get so wrapped up in something that minutes turn into hours and hours turn into, "Oh boy, I forgot to have dinner." Apparently, in his prime, Isaac Newton's mother had to regularly come in and remind him to eat because he would go entire days so absorbed in his work that he would forget.

I remember at some point I used to listen to Grant Chakoane on Metro Fm, Radio Metro then, on Sundays, wow, that guy blew me away. He would read some motivational poems and stories and was so authentic. He would laugh out loud on radio, really enjoying himself and what he was doing. He really got me excited and gave me hope too that one can do what one loves.

I remember talking to some people and some said when I talked I reminded them of Grant Chakoane and that made me feel so honoured! Almost 20 years later, I am writing articles and books as well as motivating and inspiring people.

Maybe for you, it's something else. Maybe it's organising things efficiently, or getting lost in a fantasy world, or teaching somebody something, or solving technical problems. Whatever it is, don't just look at the activities that keep you up all night, but look at the cognitive principles behind those activities that captivate you. Because they can easily be applied elsewhere.

10. How can you better embarrass yourself?

Before you are able to be good at something and do something important, you must first suck at something and have no clue what you're doing. That's pretty obvious. And in order to suck at something and have no clue what you're doing, you must embarrass yourself somehow. Most people try to avoid embarrassing themselves. If you avoid anything that could potentially embarrass you, then you will never end up doing something that feels important. Yes, it seems that once again, it all comes back to vulnerability.

Right now, there's something you want to do, something you think about doing, something you fantasise about doing, yet you don't do it. You have your reasons, no doubt. And you repeat these reasons to yourself.

But what are those reasons?

If your reasons are something like, "I can't start a business because spending time with my kids is more important to me," or "Playing Starcraft all day would probably interfere with my music, and music is more important to me," they are 100% legitimate reasons.

But if your reasons are, "My parents would hate it," or "My friends would make fun of me," or "If I failed, I'd look like an idiot," then chances are, you're actually avoiding something you truly care about because caring about that thing is what scares you, not what mom thinks or what Timmy next door says.

Living a life avoiding embarrassment is akin to living a life with your head in the sand.

Great things are, by their very nature, unique and unconventional. Therefore, to achieve them, we must go against the herd mentality. And to do that is scary. Embrace embarrassment. Feeling foolish is part of the path to achieving something important, something meaningful. The more a major life decision scares you, chances are the more you need to be doing it.

11. How are you going to save the world?

In case you haven't seen the news lately, the world has a few problems. I've harped on this before, and the research also bears it out, but to live a happy and healthy life, we must hold on to values that are greater than our own pleasure or satisfaction. So pick a problem and start saving the world. There are plenty to choose from. Our challenged education systems, economic development, domestic violence, mental health care, governmental corruption. There is always so much to do.

Find a problem you care about and start solving it. Obviously, you're not going to fix the world's problems by yourself. But you can contribute and make a difference. And that feeling of making a difference is ultimately what's most important for your own happiness and fulfilment.

12. If you had to leave the house, where would you go and what would you do?

For many of us, the enemy is complacency. We get into our routines. We distract ourselves. The couch is comfortable. The Doritos are cheesy. And nothing new happens. This is a problem. What most people don't understand is that passion is the result of action, not the cause of it.

Discovering what you're passionate about in life and what matters to you is a full-contact sport, a trial-and-error process. None of us knows exactly how we feel about an activity until we actually do the activity.

So ask yourself, if someone put a gun to your head and forced you to leave your house every day for everything except for sleep, how would you choose to occupy yourself? Let's pretend there are no useless websites, no video games, no TV. You have to be outside of the house all day every day until it's time to go to bed — where would you go and what would you do? Sign up for a dance class? Join a book club? Go get another degree? Go to church and pray? Work in an orphanage? Invent a new form of irrigation system that can save thousands of children's lives in rural Africa? What would you do with all of that time? Write down a few answers and then go out and actually do them.

13. If you knew you were going to die one year from today, what would you do and how would you want to be remembered?

Most of us don't like thinking about death. It freaks us out. But thinking about our own death has a lot of practical advantages. One of those advantages is that it forces us to zero in on what's actually important in our lives and what's just frivolous and distracting. This question makes us think about our lives in a different way and re-evaluate our priorities.

In the end, figuring out your dream, your passion, your career path or your life purpose isn't an easy process and no magic wand exists for doing it.

Think about it, pray over it, answer the above questions and you should eventually figure out what's right for you, nobody else, but you.

Tools & inspiration
Dream like a kid

"If there is no enemy within, the enemy outside can do us no harm."
Old African Proverb

The world is forever telling us to "grow up" and "take responsibility" but yet, child behaviour can be quite brilliant. Such behaviour is spectacularly good at figuring out the world and your part in it. Kids try many things.

Stupid things, like eating soil or roller-skating on ice. But they're fearless and relentless. Kids don't know what they don't know. So they question everything. Kids are easily bored. They live in fantasy worlds because present reality is limiting.

The great advantage of being an adult is that you can direct yourself. Children don't have the freedom or the awareness to steer their own development. Maybe your childhood wasn't what it could have been – but you can fix it now:

Play - The first time Ronaldo kicked a ball, he didn't foresee receiving trophies or millions of euros. If you're trying something out, don't be in too much of a hurry to take it seriously. Aim to simply enjoy. The effort will come if the passion is there.
Get reckless - If you really don't know what you want to do, you're going to have to try things you haven't done yet. And you're going to fail – a lot
– trying many different things, most of which won't work. Kids find this a lot easier because they don't worry about

consequences. I encourage you to do the same.

Question everything - Limiting beliefs like "artists can't earn a living" or "I'm not smart enough to do this", hold you back. Explore what seems to be impossible. Try some of the things you fantasised about as a child, like playing the whole day…

Listen - Children are pretty good at listening, mostly because when they don't listen they get a smack. As adults we are too busy doing 'stuff' and it prevents us from hearing our inner voice, the advice of others and the guidance of God. It's a pity there's no one to smack us; you have to smack yourself.

Some who've answered the call

"When we are no longer able to change a situation - we are challenged to change ourselves."

Victor Frankl (1905 – 1997), neurologist, psychiatrist and Auschwitz concentration camp survivor

Me, Veli

Life has taught me to remain humble irrespective of what happens. I have had situations in my life as an entrepreneur that were very humbling indeed. I have had times when I was out of pocket, without money to service my financial obligations, but let me start at the beginning.

When the world economy took a bad turn, things dried up for me in the main areas of my small business, namely staff placements and corporate training. When the economy takes strain, the market has to respond to that and recruitment and staff training become low priorities for most companies and businesses. Companies optimise the way they run business; they start doing more with less; same amount of output with less staff.

So my business took serious strain. My dream of running a successful small business came under threat. As someone who has a positive outlook on life, I didn't let this deter me. I decided it was time for me to answer the phone calls (that I had always been receiving from the banks) offering loans. I was creditworthy, I had no worries.

I remember well the day I went to the bank. I was looking good, feeling good and thinking good. I arrived at the consultant and spoke to her about either increasing my overdraft, or getting a revolving loan which I would settle in a few months. All was well and she started entering my details on the system. But then, she looked at her computer screen and said the bank was not in a position to loan me more money as my account was already in negative balance. She asked me when I would pay back the money, saying that maybe something could be worked out for the short-term. But how can any entrepreneur commit to a short-term loan repayment? I had no income-generating activities in my business at that stage, yet expenses were accumulating. I didn't get the loan.

I felt humiliated and somewhat angry that I received calls from the bank offering loans and yet, when I needed a loan the most, the bank couldn't help me. I remember leaving the bank with my tail between my legs, and I could hear the voice in my head saying, "Yes, Mr Positive, are you feeling motivated now? Are you still awesome now? Are you still feeling that you are the best thing that ever happened to this world? Are you still feeling that you have a special assignment from God?"

It was very difficult and I didn't know what to do. I remembered one of my favourite scriptures, Proverbs 16:3 which says, "Commit thy works unto Him and thy thoughts shall be established."

Have you ever realised how spiritual you become when you are in trouble? You try to cut some deals with God just for Him to let you off the hook. I felt that my world was crumbling down.

I knew people that had promised to support my small business; they had the ability to help and a need for my services and they told me never to worry about anything. But when I called them, they wouldn't pick up their phones and couldn't be there for me. The people you trust and that promise you support, sometimes let you down in a big way.

I remembered the words of my mentor Les Brown, in one of our conversations, when he said to me, "Veli, always remember that about 90% of the people you know will not support you, they will let you down when you need them most; only 10 % will support you. But there will be strangers that will believe in you and support you; when you believe in your stuff and abilities, the universe will conspire with you. It will send you supporters in the form of strangers. People will show up in your life and extend their hand to you without expecting anything in return or any favours."

These words became very true in my life. I felt very alone. It was hard to stay on course. I kept on saying, "This too shall pass", and that God cannot put you through something beyond your strength. I sat down and really had some serious introspection about my situation. I was trying to find answers.

Did it mean God did not approve of my small business and as a result he closed all the doors? There were times I couldn't sleep at night, turning and tossing and worrying about my financial situation. I continued with life as if nothing was happening, I was bold and confident that somehow it would pass, but truth be told I didn't know how. Some people envied me (seemingly a successful entrepreneur) because they didn't know the storm I was in. It was hard to keep going. I clung to my faith and used affirmations that, "Whatever I start, I finish and giving up is not an

option."
I envied people on paydays, when I saw long queues of people at bank ATMs. Why must I battle like this?, I wondered and thought about looking for employment. As an employee, I'd be guaranteed an income every month. I'd just have to give up my dream of being an entrepreneur.

It was during deep introspection that I remembered words by Hellen Keller, "When one door of happiness closes, another opens, but often we look so long at the closed door that we do not see the one that has been opened for us." This made me evaluate my situation. I started to realise that God had closed some doors for me on purpose, that He wanted me to do something else. I started looking for alternatives, checking what other doors were open to me. The door I found led to motivational talks; something I had done casually on occasion and intended doing one day in the future, not now.

Seeing that no new work came into my business, I started offering free motivational talks here and there, to schools as well as to companies. I did them as though I was being paid a million rand to do them. You cannot imagine how difficult it is to give free motivational talks when you can't service your financial obligations. I'd feel happy with the clapping and the smiles received from my audience, only to be knocked down by despair as I walked into my office to face an electricity disconnection notice from the municipality stating that I had seven days to settle my account. I went to negotiate with the municipality, but was told it was too late, I had to pay and that's that. The guy behind the desk was very cold towards me and once again I felt humiliated and small.

Somehow I made it. I kept going. In the popular animation movie 'Finding Nemo', the little silly fish Dory says, "Just keep swimming, just keep swimming." It's good advice from a little fish, let me tell you. I kept praying, picking myself up and trying again.

I kept reminding myself of Bible scriptures like Luke 12:34, "Wherever your treasure is there your heart will also be." I believe it to mean that we should not chase money treasures, but search our hearts to find our ultimate treasure which is our God-given purpose on earth. When you find and become good at doing that which your heart loves, the world rewards you for it.

This is when you attract money treasures.
Jim Rohn, an American entrepreneur, speaker and author once said, "Success is not something you pursue, but success is something you attract by becoming attractive." In other words, when you are good at what you do, the world cannot ignore you.

I became good at motivational speaking. I say this with humility, not as a boast. And motivational speaking has become my source of joy and of income. I am still an entrepreneur, I have managed to keep my dream. But now, instead of focusing on recruitment and training, I focus on inspiring others through my talks and writings. I am making a difference, albeit in a way I hadn't imagined before. There's nothing in the world that I'd rather be doing. I love motivating and inspiring people. I love people, love my job, love where I am at presently. I am grateful every second of my life for the grace of living a meaningful life, like I always dreamed of.

The reason I am sharing my personal story here is because I know that there are people going through a situation similar to mine. I want to be the one telling you not to give up hope, not to give up on your noble dreams. Remember that when one door closes, you must walk around and look for an alternative open door.

Never cease trying to be the best you can be. That's under your control. If you get too involved and concerned in things over which you have no control, it will adversely affect the thing over which you have control. Be your own person and know that you were born for a purpose and that purpose should be your daily task.

My friend Athol Nicol

It's strange how people don't like to talk about death. Many find death to be frightening and even, yes, creepy. It's not necessarily dying that scares most people, but what it means. There's no more time to hug loved ones, tell someone you love them, or share life with others. Death is powerful – but it remains one of the greatest motivators.

I have a friend who is in his deathbed, but yet continues to live a full life (as I write this in August 2016). But allow him to tell you his story himself:

"My name is Athol Nicol and am 67 years old. I have been married to my lovely wife Dot for 42 years. I am a civil engineer by profession. In 1999, I was diagnosed with prostate cancer, one of the scariest diseases in the world. I decided though that cancer would not define me. Consequently, I took up running again and completed three Comrades marathons and one Two Oceans marathon.

I remember as a young man hearing the story of Roger Bannister, the athlete who broke a record by completing a mile in less than four minutes in April 1954. This was unheard of then. Few weeks later, John Landy was able to complete it as well and thereafter many have since done so. Roger's story inspired me to challenge myself and confront my fears. I then set a goal to complete a mile as well in four minutes. That didn't happen though, I completed it in five minutes. But I was pleased with my performance and I learnt to always raise a bar on myself. Most people set the bar too low and achieve it, but lose a lot in the bigger scheme of things.

As a 67-year-old cancer sufferer, I am lying on my sick bed or call it deathbed, looking at death in the eyes without fear. I am reflecting on my life and would like to share these few things so that you may benefit from them as I can no longer move around and do what I would love to do. It's just a matter of time before I take my last breath.

My greatest regret in life: is that I didn't try hard enough to be the best that I could have been. I feel very strongly about that. My behaviour is contrary to the teaching of Christ Jesus who said, "Go forth and live an abundant life." Now I realise that success is not something you pursue, but something you attract by becoming more skilled and the best in whatever you do. Being the very best in whatever you do opens up opportunities for you to be in demand. This allows you to generate more money to take care of yourself and your family, and to save enough for the future. It's only now that I realise that I wasted a lot of life. Living a wasted life is the worst crime to commit. I also regret having smoked cigarettes as it jeopardised my health. I regret not saving enough, now all my savings are servicing the medical bills and my family won't have enough money left when I leave this planet, and I cannot fix that in any way.

How could I have been happier? I could have been happier if I had travelled the world. I did not fully apply myself in my career, as I thought everything would be fine. I did not have enough money to travel and raise my kids at the same time. I focused on raising my kids instead. If, and only if, I had applied myself to become the best in my chosen career, I would have made enough money and also found peace in what I was doing. That deprived me of so many things that I cannot fix now. If I were to live my life over again, I would strive to be the best in whatever endeavour I chose, and put my heart and soul to it. I advise you to follow your passion and not waste time doing what you don't love. That's one thing that wastes life, the Bible says in Luke 12:34, "Wherever you treasure is, there your heart will be also." Don't just follow what you studied at school, let your heart guide you and you will find that one thing that you are passionate about and pursue it with your heart and soul. This will bring peace, happiness and treasures into your life.

What would I do if I were to live my life again? If I were to have the opportunity to live my life all over again, I would pursue a study in veterinary science, a study of animals. I have realised that I always took it lightly and suppressed my passion and love for animals. Right now, I enjoy seeing and having them around me but I cannot do anything about that passion of mine anymore. I had the time but I wasted it on trivial and unnecessary things. You see you are only given one life, there are no second chances, once you leave the life you have, it's game over.

What keeps me inspired and looking forward to the next day? I am so humbled by seeing and experiencing the goodness that surrounds me. The love and support that I am receiving from my family and friends, which I cannot reciprocate. I sometimes wonder how my life could have turned out had I not been surrounded by so much love and caring. Receiving true love makes me appreciate life even more and once again I cannot return the favour except telling these wonderful people how much I appreciate their presence in my life.

Every day I say to myself, I want to live. I was admitted into Hospice as I was in terrible pain that couldn't be controlled by morphine. I was there twice in separate visits and each visit was a week long. There are two ways to leave hospice once you are admitted, alive or dead, but on both occasions I chose life and was determined. Invest your time with your family and good friends, this you will need in time like I do now.

What advice I would give the youth? Don't waste your life on trivial things and to please people. You are a gift to this world. Apply yourself fully and you will have an abundant life. Find your passion by getting involved, participating in different activities. The Bible says, "Ask and it shall be given; seek and you shall find; knock and it shall open to you." So, for me it simply means that the findings are for the seekers. You cannot find anything if you do not seek. It is the seeking that will expose you to different passions and possibilities.

I was often asked by young men, "Where do we find girls?" I always answered by saying, "Everywhere!" I do not believe there's any magic wand to answer this question. To find anything, you must search everywhere. If you want a fit and healthy partner, join a running club in your area. Always be in a receptive state, be prepared, participate and keep your eyes, ears, and heart open to any possibility.

What is my legacy? I would say that my legacy will be the principles and values that I lived by. I hope that they will continue and that the faults I made will be forgotten."

NOTE: Athol passed away on 15 October 2016, may his soul rest in peace.

My friend Rosinah Mashudu Sivhiya
Baking giant Rosinah Mashudu Sivhiya was born in the dusty rural village of Mulima, Venda, in Limpopo province, in 1967. She is the youngest sibling of the five children of the late Madiawetja Sivhiya (the first of two wives of Lebeko Abel Sivhiya).

After a troubled adolescence in a small farming community of Mamphagi, where she attended primary school, Rosinah was forced to leave this community owing to the painful divorce of her parents in the late 1970s. Subsequent to this divorce, her mother moved away from the area of Venda in trying to secure a better future for herself and the children. Rosinah was sent to stay with her aunt in the nearby community of Kutama since her mother could no longer take care of her. In between, Rosinah would stay with her other aunt in Ha-Mashamba (about 40 miles from Kutama).

She attended junior school in the village of Kutama and high school in the village of Mashamba. It was during this period that she fell in love with a local boy, Reuben Mulaudzi. Unfortunately, in 1986 (aged 19) she fell pregnant before she could complete her high school education. She later gave birth to a handsome, bouncy baby boy, Ronald.

At this point she was forced to move in with her child's father at his parents' house. She had to leave school as there was nobody willing to look after the child. Things turned for the worst while cohabiting with her child's father. She was left with no other choice, but to seek other alternatives. She sought refuge at her three sisters, moving from one end to the other as she could no longer go back to her aunts. She tried to go back to school, but the pressure to feed her child took toll on her. She needed to seek work or income-generating opportunities.

The lowest point of her life came in 1992 when she had to leave her boy in Venda in search for work in Gauteng, the so-called Place of Gold. She left him in the care of his paternal grandmother. The boy stayed with his grandmother until she died; he was 10 years old. Then he had to leave his grandmother's house to go stay with his aunt in the nearby village.

This Rosinah equates to a carbon copy of her life when her parents divorced and she also had to be content to live with relatives. Today she is working hard to ensure that Ronald's life is not defined by his difficult background, but by the desire to succeed against all odds. She has put him through school and he is well on his way to making a better life for himself.

When she arrived in Johannesburg, she sought refuge at her cousin, Elsie (a domestic worker) in Randburg. It was not long before she herself got a job as a domestic worker. Rosinah worked for the Gregory family from 1992 to 2003 in Glenvista, south of Johannesburg, until they relocated to Perth, Australia in 2003. During her stay with the Gregory family, she developed a passion for baking and cooking as this family dedicated their lives to training her for comprehensive household care, cooking and baking. When they decided to relocate to Australia, they begged her to go with them, but she could not go as she had a child who was still in school. During her tenure as an employee of this family, she began to bake and supplied the locals in Glenvista with some of her goodies.

Eventually, she began to supply local businesses with food for their functions. Due to her large network of women friends in the area, word spread to other neighbourhoods and her business started flourishing.

The Gregorys' departure meant that she had to find a place to continue with her business, but the Gregory family made it easier for her by recommending her to the Brandt family.

In 2003, she relocated to Brackenhurst, Alberton, where she started working for the Brandt family. This relocation meant that her business was going to take a dive as her clientele was now left in the South. Because of her networking ability and people skills, it did not take her long to find her niche. In fact, this proved to be the beginning of her most successful spell. She quickly built up a clientele and expanded her baking business to include that of catering. She took an advanced cooking and hospitality course. Her employer partnered with her and assisted her with marketing to local business. She also partnered with other local women to assist with baking, cooking and supplying.

She continues to service local residents as well as a number of small and medium size business in and around Alberton, Glenvista and Johannesburg CBD. Local crèches and primary schools use her to supply party packs for kids whenever there are functions like sports days, graduations and similar events. Local residents use her for children's parties. She has a natural affinity for children and they just love her.

She continues to service local residents as well as a number of small and medium size business in and around Alberton, Glenvista and Johannesburg CBD. Local crèches and primary schools use her to supply party packs for kids whenever there are functions like sports days, graduations and similar events. Local residents use her for children's parties. She has a natural affinity for children and they just love her.

In 2013, Rosinah finally registered her business called Rosanah Catering and Projects with the Companies and Intellectual Property Commission (CIPC). She now owns a big kitchen in Kibler Park where she does most of her work. Many describe her courageous achievement as humbling and inspiring to many women around the country.

She has formed a women empowerment group that focuses on developing women domestic workers in Johannesburg. She inspires them to attend workshops on how to best handle their work, entrepreneurship, investments and the broader life outlook.

She also participates in many local charity events, particularly children's homes. This is close to her heart because of her childhood, and she does not want to see any child go through what she went through.

A note on dreaming

"The future belongs to those who believe in the beauty of their dreams." Eleanor Roosevelt(October 11, 1884 – November 7, 1962), American politician, diplomat, activist and longest-serving First Lady of the United States so far

I hope you enjoy reading this book as much as I enjoyed writing it. I urge you to chase your dreams whatever they may be. If you dream of becoming a world leader – go for it. If you dream of becoming a mechanic - go for it. If you dream of helping others like Mother Theresa of Calcutta - go for it. There's no dream too high or too low. The important thing is to become the best person you can be and live life to the fullest.

But that said, I have to add that there are limitations, terms and conditions, so to speak. It is not right or acceptable to harm and hurt yourself or other people in the process of achieving your dreams. You should not look down on the dreams of others, or belittle or make fun of their dreams. Leave others' dreams alone, okay? You should also not deliberately harm any other living thing, animal or plant, or the environment.

Dreaming of taking revenge on someone, of stealing something that rightfully belongs to someone else or dreaming of destroying something that is good, are in my opinion also not acceptable. In my book, dreaming refers to noble aspirations; not to cold-hearted, selfish and cruel desires to be better than other people and have more than other people. If you come across people who do that, hey, please tell them to stop dreaming!

Acknowledgements

Firstly I would like to thank God, the Almighty for revealing my life's purpose through the scripture found in Matthew 7:7-8 King James Version (KJV): *"Ask, and it shall be given you; seek, and ye shall find; knock, and it shall be opened unto you: For every one that asketh receiveth; and he that seeketh findeth; and to him that knocketh it shall be opened."*

The above scripture helped me realise the gifts, talents and abilities known to me now that were lying dormant. All I had to do was ask, seek and knock; lo and behold they were revealed to me.

My family: My wife Mpumi Ndaba and our two lovely boys Ntokozo and Sanele Ndaba, who believe in me and stand by me no matter how wild the dream.

My late mom Ellen Ntombini Ndaba and my great aunt Cathrine Thembani Nkosi, who made me the man I am and taught me about humility and love. My late brother Sydney Ndaba, my sister Deborah Ndaba, and my brother Joshua Ndaba.

Friends and associates: James Mpele, Bangani Ngeleza, Themba Nkosi (of Impumelelo Industrial), Gordon Rolls and Carina van der Walt.

The professional team behind this book: Eulália Snyman and Dylan Fourie.

My mentors: Les Brown, Vincent Toran, Sofia Tasker and Ronnie Martin. All the people that have made a contribution and have helped to shape the person

I have become, thank you, thank you! Thank you Lord Yaweh. I love you all. I thank everyone from the bottom of my heart.

To you reading this book – blessings.

Veli Ndaba 2016

References and suggested reading

You Are Born to Win – by Veli Ndaba

The Essence of Success – by Earl Nightingale

Your Daily WOW – by Melissa West

In Search of Excellence – by Thomas J. Peters and Robert H. Waterman, Jr

I write I what I like – by Steve Biko

It's Not How Good You Are, It's How Good You Want To Be – By Paul Arden

You Tube Book Summaries – by Brian Johnson

Man's Search for Meaning – by Viktor Frankl

The Holy Bible

Awaken the Giant Within – by Tony Robbins

What On Earth Am I Here For? – by Rick Warren

The Measure of a Man – by Sydney Poitier

Own your Industry – by Douglas Kruger

Long Walk to Freedom – by Nelson Mandela

It's Not Over Until You Win: How to become the person you always wanted to be no matter what the obstacle – by Les Brown

The Greatest Salesman in the World – by OG Mandino

www.ingramcontent.com/pod-product-compliance
Lightning Source LLC
Chambersburg PA
CBHW030942090426
42737CB00007B/505